Edgar Cayce and the Unfulfilled Destiny of Thomas Jefferson Reborn

By Joanne DiMaggio

For permission, or serialization, condensation, adaptions, or for our catalog of other publications, write to: Ozark Mountain Publishing, Inc., P.O. Box 754, Huntsville, AR 72740, ATTN: Permissions Department

Library of Congress Cataloging-in-Publication Data
Edgar Cayce and the Unfulfilled Destiny of Thomas Jefferson Reborn by Joanne DiMaggio -1950-

This book is the result of one such journey - a long and winding road for two souls fated to be united to fulfill a pre-life agreement.

1. Spiritual 2. Karma 3. Past Lives 4. Metaphysical
I. DiMaggio, Joanne, 1950 II. Metaphysical III. Past Lives IV. Title

Library of Congress Catalog Card Number: 2020939797
ISBN: 9781940265872

Cover Art and Layout: Victoria Cooper Art
Book set in: Times New Roman, Bell MT
Book Design: Summer Garr

Published by:

PO Box 754, Huntsville, AR 72740
800-935-0045 or 479-738-2348; fax 479-738-2448
WWW.OZARKMT.COM
Printed in the United States of America

For T.J.
A promise kept

Yet if there are the developments through the environs, it may be seen that this entity - [1208] - may become more important in the affairs of the world than this entity in its previous experience has been to America - Thomas Jefferson (1208-1, T2).

Acknowledgments

There are two individuals who played a major role in creating this book. The first, of course, is T.J. Davis, who so willingly shared the enchantment of his life when Edgar Cayce was in it, and the struggles he encountered after Cayce died. Being able to work with someone who lived with and was so loved by Cayce was a gift of unimaginable joy. His memories have served as the nucleus around which this book was built and I am humbled that the Universe saw fit to bring us together again in this life for this common purpose.

When it came to the nitty-gritty of pulling the information together, my deepest appreciation goes to Karen Davis of the Edgar Cayce Foundation (ECF). I learned a great deal from Karen—not just about the complexities of using archived material, but also about the greater purpose in sharing this with an audience. Like Gladys Davis, Karen served as the gatekeeper for ECF, being actively involved in making sure the delicate material I was so ardently studying was handled in a way to optimize its preservation. But more importantly, as a member of the Davis family, Karen was fiercely protective of the integrity of the Cayce and Davis families, of the

Association for Research and Enlightenment (A.R.E.), the Cayce Work, and the manner in which I portrayed those who played a role in T.J.'s story. We spent hours together discussing how to present this material and I took her gentle and loving counsel to heart every step of the way. Her thoughtful perspective and non-wavering support held me—and this project—together. She is truly a treasure and I am grateful for every moment we spent together.

I would also like to thank Laura Hoff of ECF, who vetted the readings in a timely fashion; Stephanie Pope, who so graciously gave of her time and expertise to provide constructive criticism of the manuscript; PMH Atwater, for her support and leading me to the Authors Guild for invaluable advice; and Lisa Ellison, who guided me into exploring several options on how to rework the content. I also want to acknowledge some of my early manuscript readers, especially Toni Romano, who provided invaluable input. My appreciation goes to John Aguilar, who graciously allowed me to use the photo he took of T.J. wearing Edgar Cayce's hat. And finally, my love and thanks to Day Schwartz, who was always there cheering me on, and to everyone else in my circle of friends and colleagues who patiently and lovingly listened to my doubts about this project and somehow managed to keep my spirits lifted so I could see it through to the end. You are all magical human beings!

Contents

Edgar Cayce and the Unfulfilled Destiny of Thomas Jefferson Reborn
Published by: Ozark Mountain Publishing

Soul Writing: Conversing With Your Higher Self
Published by: Self-Published – Olde Souls Press

Your Soul Remembers: Accessing Your Past Lives Through Soul Writing
Published by: Rainbow Ridge Books

Karma Can BE a Real Pain: Past Life Clues to Current Life Maladies
Published by: Rainbow Ridge Books

I Did It To Myself…Again! New Life-Between-Lives Case Studies Show How Your Soul's Contract is Guiding Your Life
Published by: Balboa Press

OZARK
MOUNTAIN
PUBLISHING

For more information about any of the above titles, soon to be released titles, or other items in our catalog, write, phone or visit our website:
Ozark Mountain Publishing, Inc.
PO Box 754, Huntsville, AR 72740
479-738-2348/800-935-0045
www.ozarkmt.com

Preface

Life is full of ironies: those unexpected twists and turns that are part of your soul's journey. This book is the result of one such journey—a long and winding road for two souls fated to be united to fulfill a pre-life agreement.

I am, by nature, a truth seeker: a scribe whose mission is to uncover and shed light on the people, places, and events that are otherwise silenced. I sense over the years I have perfected my role as a reporter for the Universe, acquiring specialized gifts to enable me to do the work for which I am entrusted. One of those gifts is soul recognition.

The veil between lives has never existed for me. I don't experience life as something segmented into past, present, and future. Edgar Cayce, the most renowned and researched psychic of the twentieth century, who founded the Association for Research and Enlightenment in Virginia Beach, said life is continuous, and I operate under that premise. So, it is that when I encounter a soul that I recognize, my first instinct is to find a way to assist him or her on its present life journey. More often than not, it means being a witness to the truth of who they are, recording that truth, and sharing it with others. If I can resolve some of my own karma along the way, all the better!

I first heard of #1208—the number assigned to Thomas Jefferson (T.J.) Davis in the Cayce readings—in 1987. I was fascinated by what I read about him, and as any intuitive reporter looking for a good story, I felt compelled to interview him for a possible feature article. I knew very little about him at this early juncture, but what little I knew—that when he was two days old, Edgar Cayce gave him a life reading and in it said he was the reincarnation of Alexander the Great and Thomas Jefferson—was enough to peak my curiosity about how his life had turned out. What was it like to have had such an auspicious life reading as a baby? It had to have impacted him in a major way, and I wondered whether that information made his life easier, or whether the burden of such knowledge made it a living hell.

I did what I could to reach him, but despite my repeated efforts, it took nine years before our paths would cross. The details of all that transpired during those nine years are not pertinent for this book. Suffice to say, the odds were stacked against us. There were numerous people who were in a position of connecting us, but instead did everything in their power to prevent our meeting during those pivotal years. Whenever I would broach the subject, I received one stern warning after the other to stay away from him.

These red flags were being waved by people I knew and respected: people who knew T.J. years before

I came on the scene. They had that advantage over me, but no one ever revealed what he did to make them so adamant about us not meeting. There were hints about his irresponsible lifestyle and his womanizing. He was likened to a hippy beach bum who took advantage of people to get what he wanted. Even today, there are people who react with disdain at the mere mention of his name. I am not naïve and did not go into this project thinking he walked on water simply because Cayce said he had been Alexander or Jefferson. On the contrary, I knew his life choices contributed to what many believed was a much-deserved bad-boy reputation. Yet despite the well-intentioned warnings I received to not become involved with him, I continued to harbor this inexplicable nagging feeling I had that there was some unfinished business between us—that we may have shared previous lifetimes together and that I was the one to best tell his story.

I often found myself wondering why I felt that way, especially when circumstances conspired to keep us apart. In 1987, I asked this of a well-respected psychic who told me if we were meant to meet, nothing I would do would stop it from happening. On the other hand, if it wasn't meant to be, there wasn't anything I could do to make it happen. Free will notwithstanding, it was pretty much up to the Universe whether our paths would ever cross.

Over the next few years I tried to put it out of my mind and kept busy helping establish the A.R.E. Heartland Region in Chicago while simultaneously running PLEXUS, a past-life research, education, and therapy organization I had founded. The latter gave me the opportunity to meet individuals on the cutting edge of regression therapy and thus further my research into how men and women's past lives were impacting their present lives.

In meeting like-minded souls through the A.R.E. and PLEXUS, T.J.'s name invariably came up, and with synchronicity at play, I continued to stumble upon individuals who knew him. Some of them were sympathetic and thought at the very least that I should have the opportunity to meet him. Yet despite their intervention, an actual meeting never occurred. At times, it seemed that the Universe was playing a game, constantly putting the carrot before me with absolutely no intention of allowing me to take a bite. I wondered if this wasn't some sort of cosmic joke.

In 1995 I moved to Charlottesville, Virginia, to start a publishing company, which never got off the ground. Nonetheless, as I had fallen in love with Charlottesville when I first visited in the early '70s, I decided to stay. When I arrived, I had no idea that T.J. also had moved to Charlottesville, and was living a mere thirteen miles away. I had pretty much put him out of my mind and instead focused on meeting like-minded souls in my new community so I could make friends and pursue my career as a writer and past-life therapist.

One of the first things I did was to contact a fellow member of the now-disbanded Association for Past Life

Research and Therapies (APRT). They had a directory of past-life therapists across the country, and looking in Virginia, I found a contact in Charlottesville. I decided to introduce myself to see if he'd be interested in starting a past-life study group in Charlottesville. Shortly after our conversation, he called back to say he had told his colleague about me, as we had similar interests. She wondered if I would accept an invitation to come to her home for dinner as a way of welcoming me to Charlottesville. I was flattered and said I would be happy to accept. He said she'd call me to issue the formal invitation, and sure enough, a short time later the phone rang. She introduced herself and then said the words that would change my life forever. She said she and her husband, T.J. Davis, would like to invite my children and me to their home for dinner the following Saturday.

Her husband, T.J. Davis? I must have zoned out because I don't remember what I said, other than to accept her invitation. When the full realization of what was happening settled in, my heart was beating so rapidly that I had to sit down. I had vowed not to look for T.J. and had come to terms with the fact that it was unlikely we'd ever meet. So many people had put roadblocks in place to make sure this did not happen that I had long since accepted it as the Universe's way of safeguarding me from an unpleasant encounter of the karmic kind. Now I learn he is living in the same town and I'm being invited to his home for dinner?

After the initial shock wore off, I had to smile.

This was divine orchestration at play. I remembered the words I heard ten years earlier—that I could do nothing to make something happen if it *wasn't* meant to be and that I could do nothing to stop it from happening if it *was* meant to be. Clearly our meeting *was* meant to be.

So, it was in late January 1996, with dessert and my children in the backseat, I drove to T.J.'s rustic farmhouse that sat midway up a rough mountain road. I nervously approached the door, not knowing what in the world awaited me. After having gone through so many years of being kept apart, I thought bells would go off and the earth would open up and swallow us whole. Neither happened. When we met, my anxiety abated and I found myself sitting in his living room, filled with a warm feeling, just like wearing comfortable slippers in front of a roaring fire on a winter's eve. I did not tell him that I already knew about his two famous past lives, but it didn't matter because before the evening ended, he willingly revealed his identity to me.

Our friendship blossomed in the coming weeks. Ever mindful of my assignment, by late March I broached the subject of writing his biography and was thrilled when he said he was open to the idea. We continued talking for months about this project, but after a while, something changed. We unexpectedly began to grow apart, and our conversations became sporadic at best. Months later when he called to say he and his wife had separated, I knew he was preoccupied with the new direction his life was going. I also knew it was highly unlikely that we would ever get around to writing his memoirs.

My last conversation with T.J. before what would become a nine-year separation was in October 2000. A few weeks later, I was involved in a near-fatal automobile accident that profoundly changed my life with repercussions that would last for years. Something happened to me at the moment of impact that I now know was a near-death experience (NDE). In the weeks following the accident, I found myself retreating from the life I had led up until that point in time. I didn't realize what was happening at first, but I began losing all desire to pursue past-life research. Anything remotely metaphysical no longer interested me, and that included the people associated with it—especially people like T.J. Davis.

On March 30, 2001, my dear mother died. She lived in Phoenix and I had spent the last few months flying back and forth to see her. Between my automobile accident and her death, my heart and soul endured two life-altering traumas within months of each other.

After her funeral, I returned to Charlottesville, and for reasons I still don't understand, I began dismantling my life. I disbanded PLEXUS, distanced myself from the A.R.E., gave away most of my metaphysical library (something I came to regret), and cut off all communication with anyone and everyone that had to do with the life I lived prior to the accident. For all intents and purposes, I was suffering from a kind of spiritual amnesia. I remembered everything and everyone from the past, but those memories no longer had an emotional charge. I just didn't care anymore.

For the next three years, I lived in an emotionally detached state, which I later discovered is a common side effect of an NDE. I was functioning and no one around me knew anything was different. I remained in this spiritual limbo until November 9, 2003—the third anniversary of the accident. That morning I awoke to find myself "back" to the person I was before the accident occurred—all the emotional ties to the past restored. This was all well and good, but by then everyone and everything associated with my previous life was long gone.

Over the next three years (everything seemed to be happening in threes), I desperately worked on recovering my former life, trying to understand what had happened and how I could reconnect with the like-minded friends I had pushed away. T.J. was not included on that list, as I was certain our time was long over.

Unfortunately, I was unsuccessful at rekindling the friendships I had with those I cared about before. As a result, I became despondent. My health deteriorated and my energies were spread thin as I tried to hold down a full-time job and still make frequent trips to Phoenix to care for my now-ailing father. During one of those visits in 2004, I began having symptoms of a heart attack and found myself in an ICU. As it turned out, I did not have a heart attack, but I did have to undergo a cardiac procedure. Being alone in that hospital room—two thousand miles from home, family, and friends—was the loneliest point of my life. It also helped put everything in perspective.

Still, it wasn't until after my father passed away in 2006 that I decided to do something to turn my life around. I enrolled in Atlantic University and started working on my master's in Transpersonal Studies (now called Transpersonal Psychology) degree. The coursework was a godsend. It slowly reimmersed me in the esoteric studies that were once the foundation of my life. As I felt stronger and more confident, I eased back into the work of my soul.

In 2009, I organized an A.R.E. area team in Charlottesville and rented space for our monthly programs at the local Unity Church. Although I was intrigued about Unity, I was hesitant to become involved as a congregant. Their rental coordinator was relentless, however, and kept encouraging me to attend Sunday services, which I eventually began doing in March 2009. A few months later, I was startled to see T.J. standing in the church lobby. I did not know whether to approach him or to pretend he wasn't there. I opted for the latter and circumvented him in the hope he would not see me. Besides, I told myself, even if he did glance my way, it had been nine years since we last saw each other and chances were that he wouldn't recognize me. I managed to leave the church undetected.

I worried about running into him again, but when that did not happen over the course of the next few Sundays, I realized he was not a regular churchgoer. I was relieved, but nonetheless could not help but think about him again. I mused, isn't this odd? For the last nine years I never ran into him and now here he was. Was divine orchestration in play once again? If so, for what purpose? Was I being held to my assignment to record T.J.'s life story?

It didn't take long for me to find out. On Wednesday, July 15, 2009, I was in an outlying area where I was unable to get cell phone service. As I headed home, I saw that I had two voice mail messages. I listened to the first in disbelief.

"I was just looking through my Cayce magazine I just got in the mail and I saw in Virginia you're listed in Charlottesville. I live here, too, and I was just wondering what's going on with the Search for God Group or whatever. I was just interested. My name is T.J. Davis and my phone number is . . ."

I had to play it several times. Obviously, he did not know whom he was calling. I went on to the second message. It was T.J. again. "Joanne, I just called you a few minutes ago," he laughed. "My name is T.J. I saw you in *Venture Inward* under Charlottesville as the contact person for A.R.E. And then I went on line and there was all this stuff on Unity Church and I go to Unity. At first I thought your name was familiar and I couldn't place it. And I thought just Joe DiMaggio and I thought no, that wouldn't be right. But I think I might even know who you are so if I don't hear from you I'm going to look you up Sunday."

Despite the fact that he had finally put two-and-two together, I decided not to return his call. Two days later, he called a third time. "Joanne, this is T.J. I'm just calling to see if you feel like communicating. The deal is I had a dream about you last night, but I can't remember any of it. So, I thought I better call you anyway just to see what's going on. Well, I guess that's it. Call me if you want when you get home. I'll be up until at least twelve."

His persistence convinced me to return his call, and upon hearing my voice, he seemed genuinely excited to reconnect. We had a brief conversation. I told him I was hosting an A.R.E. program the next day—ironically on NDE—and invited him to be my guest. He agreed.

The following day while I was setting up for the program, I kept my eye on the door wondering if he would show up. When I saw him standing in line, I walked up to him, tugged his sleeve, and pulled him out of line. It felt good to reconnect.

He sat through the program, but left immediately after it was over without saying goodbye. As I drove home, I saw that he left another message. "Joanne, I was so impressed with what you've done. I just wanted to call you up and tell you. That was just wonderful. And I'm sorry I ran out after the thing was over. I am just so used to being reclusive that I just hightail it the minute I see a chance, but I should have stuck around a little bit. But again, as an old friend of Mr. Cayce's, I gotta tell you he's really proud of you and what you've done. So, keep up the good work, girl. I'll talk to you later. I'll see you at church tomorrow."

True to his word, we met at church the next day and had a chance to talk after services. There was so much to say, so much to catch up on. In the back of my mind, I worried this was just another brief encounter so I told myself not to invest too heavily in our friendship as he'd no doubt disappear on me again. But there was something different about him this time. He said he had a dream that his aunt, Gladys Davis, and Edgar Cayce appeared, telling him now was the time to come forward and do the work he was meant to do. I knew what that was and I knew that had weighed on him his whole life. It was one thing to be told you were Thomas Jefferson in a past life, but in that same reading, Cayce said T.J. could do in this life for the world what Jefferson had done for this country. That was an even heavier burden to carry. After all, how do you live up to that? Already in his seventies, T.J. confided that he worried he would never fulfill that prediction. I reminded him that he was around the same age that Jefferson was when he began work on the University of Virginia, so yes, there was still time.

Of all he shared, it was his comment that Mr. Cayce would be proud of me that meant more than anything anyone had said in a long time, and coming from T.J., who grew up in the Cayce household, it was especially meaningful. Although I thought my reason for wanting to write about him was to explore what his life was like in the shadow of the Alexander/Jefferson lifetimes, I soon realized that it was his connection to Edgar Cayce—and not his glorious past lives—that was of primary importance and the real reason we were reunited. I wasn't meant to write a biography of a man who had famous past lives; I was meant to write a biography of a man who, as a young boy, was Edgar Cayce's beloved protégé.

I asked him if he was willing to talk about his years with Mr. Cayce. I knew that A.R.E. members would be fascinated by his firsthand account of life in the Cayce household. With so few people left who actually knew Mr. Cayce, T.J.'s perspective as a young child witnessing such phenomenal events, meeting so many fascinating people, and being tutored by the great master himself as they sat fishing on the pier, would be mesmerizing to audiences. Again, I brought up the idea of putting those memories in a book. He agreed, and we spent the next few weeks planning how to make this a reality.

On September 13, 2009, I hosted the first of several "Remembering Edgar Cayce: Conversations with T.J. Davis" at Unity of Charlottesville. T.J. was nervous at first, but once he settled in and realized he was among souls where it was safe to say even the most outlandish things, he began to tell his life story. As predicted, audiences hung on his every word.

The material in this book began as a compilation of the talks T.J. gave, of the additional interviews I did with him to fill in the blanks, and of my research into the Cayce readings on T.J. and those closest to him, including his parents. Most of all, it includes information contained in the numerous letters, notes, cards, and reports in his family's massive file in the Edgar Cayce Foundation archives. Working closely with Karen Davis, who is related to T.J. through marriage and who worked at ECF, the book began to take on a life of its own. Karen thought it was important that I study the files of T.J.'s family, including his beloved aunt Gladys Davis, his mother Burlynn Davis, his father Boyd Davis, who was Gladys's brother, his grandmother, and anyone else whose reading made mention of #1208. After I arranged with ECF to get permission from T.J. to study his personal file and that of his family, I started this long and arduous task, coming to Virginia Beach to work a few days at a time whenever I could afford to get away. As I painstakingly went through each paper in what seemed like endless files, the book began to evolve. Karen and I talked about the optimal way to present this material and decided it was best if it was based on the historical documentation in the file. My challenge was to bring alive the energy of that time.

To do that, the first part of the book describes what life was like in Virginia Beach in 1936–1945 during T.J.'s years with Mr. Cayce. What was the state of the world he was growing up in as families struggled to come out of the Depression only to be plunged into World War II? What was it like growing up with alcoholic parents who had gambling and health issues, were constantly on the move, never being able to hold on to a steady job to provide a family framework in which to raise a young boy? What was the true nature of the relationship between Edgar Cayce and T.J. in this and previous lifetimes? What did the master see in the student and what did the student see in the master?

At times the information I uncovered was difficult

to read. While it was a historian's treasure trove and brought to life that time and those people, it was hard to remain objective. After a while, I came to know these souls as if they were still alive. Having the unfair advantage of knowing full well what was ahead, I wanted to warn them that their decisions and their behavior would have serious consequences on T.J. At some point, I knew I had to detach from them, realizing that my job as a reporter was to give a nonjudgmental, objective accounting of what really happened and allow the readers to come to their own conclusions. I have often described myself as a "reporter for the Universe." I view my role as a scribe: to listen, record, and put words and thoughts of those I am writing about into some semblance of order and then share that with those led to pick up my book. That is why I chose to quote from the letters they exchanged so you could hear the voices of Edgar, Gladys, Boyd, and Burlynn and experience their joys, sorrows, anxieties, and fears in a way only they could convey.

My research gave me a broader understanding of the time and the intent of those around T.J. who were entrusted with his well-being. My request to you as the reader is twofold. One, to think of the first part of the book as setting the stage for what happened to T.J. later in life through the lens of the historical documentation of that time and that place and the influence it had on those around him. And second, when reading the second part of the book, to remember that T.J.'s personal reflections, memories, and perception of his childhood are based on what he believes happened. The truth is, in the course of my research, at times I found either conflicting versions of his stories, or no proof whatsoever. It's important to remember his recollection of his early life came from the vantage point of seventy-plus years later and who among us can honestly say that at eighty we could accurately relay events when we were preschoolers? Psychological studies have shown that people can recall events that never happened, that all memories are inaccurate to some degree, and identifying false memories may be next to impossible. For these reasons, I have relied on what I found in the ECF archives to serve as my truth benchmark, while still presenting T.J.'s recollection of the time he spent in the Cayce household and pertinent events after Cayce's death.

My purpose is to present documented events that shaped the lives of both the Davis and Cayce families where T.J.'s upbringing was concerned, which includes taking into consideration their past lives and the path his soul family took when reincarnating together in his current lifetime. This is especially true of T.J. himself, as all his life he has had to endure the harsh criticism that he did not fulfill the destiny Cayce said could be his. How could the former soul of Thomas Jefferson experience the lackluster life he has had as T.J. Davis? As Cayce often cited in the thousands of life readings he gave, souls gain and souls lose in any given lifetime. It is not always an upward climb where you continue to outdo what you have done before. Karmic patterns arise that must be met within self, and as his readings reveal, T.J. has had his share of interpersonal challenges to resolve during this lifetime.

Nonetheless, I have chosen to focus on what I believe to be the undeniable truth of his life: a seasoned soul chosen for a greater purpose, the struggle and beautiful synchronicity of his journey to earth to be with a most beloved mentor, his years of being the vessel into which that mentor poured the wisdom of humanity, and the free will's series of twists and turns that created the obstacles to that purpose for which he felt powerless to overcome. It is a classic case of karma in action—of synchronistic events that make one cringe to think how close and yet how far he was from achieving the destiny Edgar Cayce foresaw for his young charge. It is a sad story that is, nonetheless, filled with hope, for you will see after reading about his journey, that there is always time to fulfill that destiny.

This has been an eight-year odyssey for me, and at times, I became disillusioned to the point of not writing and putting the manuscript on a shelf for months at a time. But then some auspicious event would occur, and I'd be drawn back to the book, rewriting it over and over until this divinely led version appeared. At times, I felt alone on this journey, but at other times, I felt as though Edgar and Gladys were in the room with me, giving me that much-needed second wind to keep going. As I poured over the letters that were exchanged by this extraordinary soul family, I realized that Gladys made copies of each letter and lovingly put them away in a file, years before

I was born. It was as if she and Edgar knew that some seventy years later, the Universe would be sending one of its reporters to dig deep, stay true, and tell the story that they were unable to share in their own lifetimes.

As I continued with my research, it became apparent to me that Edgar and Gladys were engaged in a constant tug-of-war with Boyd and Burlynn over T.J.'s soul. Sometimes they won. Sometimes they lost. But in-between was a story of two families whose karmic paths became entwined once this soul came into their lives—again. This is the story of a soul family and how their interactions and decisions created the reality that became T.J.'s life. It is not sugarcoated in any way. I leave it to you to come to your own conclusion about the fate of the baby that Edgar Cayce so loved and predicted could be the world's redemption—if only. Whether or not you can identify with the conflicts this family experienced, there is no denying that T.J. was Edgar Cayce's "precious boy."

As for my friendship with Thomas Jefferson Davis, I can honestly say I am one of the few souls who has seen and experienced both sides of him, so I have no illusions about him whatsoever. After all, this isn't our first lifetime together and it probably won't be our last. Our conversations have been extraordinary at times. When I think of him now, I am reminded of what President John F. Kennedy said during an address on April 29, 1962, welcoming a group of Nobel Prize winners to a dinner in their honor at the White House. "I think this is the most extraordinary collection of talent, of human knowledge, that has ever been gathered together at the White House—with the possible exception of when Thomas Jefferson dined alone."

Thomas Jefferson indeed.

—*Joanne DiMaggio*

Note Going Forward

Those of you who are unfamiliar with the Cayce readings may find some of the coding confusing, but when you understand how these readings were identified, you'll find it an exciting process to go into the Cayce archives and review the entire reading. When one of the Cayce readings appears in the book, the first set of numbers represents the correspondent whose identity is kept confidential; the second set of numbers indicate which reading I am referencing; that is, 1208-03 would be T.J. Davis and his third reading. (For the purposes of this book, I have been given permission to share T.J.'s reading number.) When reviewing a reading, you will generally see a T, an R, or a B. T = text, representing the text of the actual reading document, and I use that reference throughout the book. R = report, copy that is based on actual correspondence; that is, excerpts of letters from Edgar Cayce and staff to recipients of readings. B = background; a mix of recorded notes or excerpts of correspondence related to how that person came into contact with Edgar Cayce for that particular reading.

In addition to the readings, which are available to

the public to review, this book also relies on the historic documents from the archives that are not open to public viewing without permission. These documents are included to illuminate the actual circumstances as they occurred in time with the people who shared a significant relationship with T.J. They are reproduced exactly as they were written without editing, so any punctuation or grammatical errors are not an oversight on our part, but an exact representation of the historic document from which they were quoted.

Part One

"A Channel of Hope and Blessings"

Chapter One

1935–1936: Finding Mr. Cayce

Edgar Cayce with T.J. Davis, age eleven months, May 1937. (ECF#0966u)

When Thomas Jefferson Davis was two days old, he was brought to the home of Edgar Cayce, the most respected and celebrated psychic of all time. T.J.—as he later was nicknamed—had the privilege of living on and off in the Cayce household for the first eight years, seven months of his life. Those years were filled with enchantment. The things he saw, the people he met, and what he experienced in that magical, mystical bubble he called home, gave him a unique perspective on life. But so did the circumstances of his birth—the biological parents he chose who were dealing with alcohol and gambling issues, as well as the country's historical time frame, still reeling from the economic consequences of the Depression while barreling into a world war.

As a very young child, it never occurred to T.J. that everyone else's life was any different from the life he knew in Mr. Cayce's Virginia Beach home at 308 Arctic Crescent. It wasn't until he was older that he began to wonder how he ended up being raised by his aunt, Gladys Davis, Edgar Cayce's secretary, and by the Cayces rather than by his parents, Thomas Boyd Davis and Burlynn Latham Davis. Like any child with a natural curiosity, he went to the one person he knew would tell him the truth. He asked Edgar Cayce.

"We just had completed a long discussion about death and the afterlife and from what he shared, he must have felt I was old enough to understand how the concept of reincarnation played a role in my arriving at his doorstep," T.J. recalled.

The lessons T.J. learned from Edgar usually came in the form of a story and the tale of how he came to live with him was no exception.

"He began by telling me that all things are possible," T.J. explained. "He said all souls reside in heaven—a word that a child my age understood—which is a very busy place. People are coming and going all the time, reviewing their past lives and trying to find a suitable karmic-related place to be reborn so they can be with the same folks they were with before."

T.J. paraphrased what he remembered Cayce telling him at the time. "You probably spotted me as a child putting my book under the pillow and learning its contents and thought that was cool. So you started paying attention to me and realized you wanted to come here and be with me when you're born."

T.J. was certain the reason his soul was looking for Edgar was because they, along with Gladys, had shared many lifetimes together. From the youngest age, he understood that he was part of Cayce's soul family and nothing, and no one, would ever shake that belief.

"I did not know it then, but later discovered this was true," he said. "I may not have remembered who I was in those lifetimes, but I knew I was there with them. Even if we weren't together physically, at least one of us was in spirit guiding the other, as was the case with Gladys, who was my guardian angel in at least one of my lifetimes."

Whatever lifetimes T.J. had, it seemed as if Gladys and Edgar were there, something Gladys reassured T.J. of on numerous occasions. So, there they were again in this twentieth-century lifetime, with Gladys in the position of being Edgar's archivist.

As he grew older, T.J. became more interested in the phenomenon of how people came to the earth. From Edgar he learned souls usually incarnated with people they were involved with in the past in order to work out karma. As T.J. put it, "You return to earth to straighten out as many of your past mistakes as you can. Many times it is not possible to do that, but nonetheless you still get a plan to work on when you're coming in."

Edgar had a plan and T.J. knew he was an integral part of it. To that end his soul was determined to find a way to the Cayce doorstep, regardless of who his biological parents were and the circumstances of his birth.

Edgar described T.J.'s search for him and Gladys as if the boy's soul were observing them on a giant celestial screen. T.J.'s soul knew it had to time its approach to the earth to correspond with the alignment of the planets so everything would be in place for it to find its way to Cayce's home.

"So, my soul did notice this kid in Kentucky who could sleep on a book and know everything and I knew that was Mr. Cayce," T.J. said. "I wanted to join him the moment I found him, but I couldn't come in right then and there because I didn't want to share a childhood with him in Kentucky. I decided to wait until he was older and had a wife and come in then as one of his children, preferably as his son."

Since there is no time in spirit, T.J. explained that he didn't realize that so many earth years passed by the time he looked in on Edgar again. "By then he had moved to a home on Arctic Crescent in Virginia Beach, which was the original A.R.E. Somehow, I had to get there so I could be in his family, but my timing was a little off and he was already too old to have any more children. I realized then I couldn't get in through his biological family."

The only alternate route was through Gladys. "I was more than willing to come in that way, but there was one small catch," T.J. said. "She wasn't married and having any children. Then a lightbulb went off. Of course! Why didn't I think of this sooner? I could come through Boyd and Burlynn Davis. Boyd was Gladys's brother. In that way, I would be Gladys's nephew and I'd have access to Mr. Cayce through her."

It seemed like an ingenious plan, because T.J. never considered that having Boyd and Burlynn as parents would prevent him from being with Edgar. After all, both of his future parents had a drinking problem—the result of their chosen lifestyle and the company they kept in the gambling world. Rather than perceiving their drinking as a negative, T.J. saw it as working in his favor. Since they were both alcoholics, he was sure they would neither want nor be able to raise him, and it would be a simple transition from them to Gladys to Mr. Cayce. This turned out to be true. The last thing Boyd and Burlynn wanted was a baby.

Boyd Davis was born February 27, 1911, in Oklahoma City, Oklahoma. Gladys asked Edgar Cayce to give a reading for her brother in 1927, hoping it would help Boyd discover his life's work. In that first reading,

Cayce said in a previous life Boyd had been Sam Davis (1842–1863), a Confederate soldier who was executed by the Union army when he would not turn informer. Sam is purported to have said, "I would rather die a thousand deaths than betray my cause."

Sam Davis was twenty-one when he died a martyr and to this day is considered a Confederate hero, as evidenced by a monument dedicated to him on the grounds of the state capitol in Nashville, Tennessee. T.J. found it interesting that his father had the same last name in his last two lifetimes. Cayce said in that lifetime Boyd's soul gained from that experience, as his actions were considered honorable and worthy of positive karma.

Gladys recounted an interesting aspect of the karmic tie-in between both lives, telling T.J. that when his father was four or five years old, he had a young African American friend by the name of Sam—the same first name that Boyd had in the Civil War lifetime. The boys were inseparable until Sam died about a year later, leaving Boyd inconsolable. Gladys told T.J. that Boyd was never close to a playmate again. Considering that Sam died so young, and that Boyd's father died when Boyd was just thirteen, Gladys commented to T.J. that it was strange that those closest to his father were taken from him in both lifetimes. T.J. wondered if that was a foretelling of his birth and then being taken away days later.

Sam Davis wasn't Boyd's only adventurous lifetime. According to Cayce, in an earlier life, Boyd accompanied Christopher Columbus and was among those who raised a flag in what is now Puerto Rico. In that lifetime, Boyd's soul lost, in that he gratified his own wishes rather than do something for the good of those who depended on him. T.J. speculated that this may be why in his life as Sam Davis, Boyd put the interest of others ahead of his own and ultimately wiped out some of the negative karma from the Columbus-era life.

There is an interesting parallel between Boyd and T.J.'s past lives. Each went out to settle new worlds. During the adventuresome Columbus lifetime, Boyd went by the name Cololon, sailing the seas to find new lands. In T.J.'s Atlantis lifetime, his name was Sululon and he helped populate several areas around the world with former Atlanteans.

Another karmic connection between father and son is that Boyd also had an Atlantean lifetime. His name then was Ellien and Cayce said he was there at the same time as T.J. when Atlantis was being destroyed. He described Ellien, however, as " . . . among those who served in the council of the ruler, and the entity then attained position, power, pomp, glory. Physically and mentally the entity was the peer of the councillors, and the entity applied same well and aright! In the urge as is seen from same, that deep desire for the right in the high and ennobling way, yet ever is this tempered by self's domination through application of conditions for self" (391-1, T15).

Between the Atlantis and the Columbus lifetimes, Boyd was called Uylessi and was director of the Grecian Olympic games. This is where his love of sports was rooted. As a senior at Selma High School in Selma, Alabama, he listed athletic director as his pet ambition.

After graduation in June 1928, he started what would become a very long list of jobs he'd hold over his lifetime. He complained about every job he had, saying the work was too hard, the hours too long, or that it just wasn't exciting enough. He fantasized about taking up aviation or playing ball or getting a job at sea. He wanted to experience a variety of cultures and people so he could learn what life was all about.

His entrance into the food business started in April 1930 when he and a friend operated a hamburger and hotdog stand in Virginia Beach. Mr. E. N. "Jim" MacWilliams, who wanted to help struggling young athletes, had given Boyd money to get started at MacWilliams's alma mater, Ohio University in Athens. Boyd was supposed to work part-time until he could get settled into the athletic program and MacWilliams offered to help further when needed.

School started on September 22, 1930, but within a week, Boyd was having second thoughts accepting any more money from MacWilliams. He felt his place was to be at home helping to support his mother and siblings and chastised himself for not considering the ramifications before going to school.

He continued to be in flux in terms of a business prospect, but by 1932, his thoughts were focused on finding the appropriate life partner, something he asked Cayce about in another of his readings. In finding that companion, he had to look no further than his past life as Uylessi for that is where he met the soul who eventually became T.J.'s mother. Her name then was Arcelus and she helped to establish the games in both Greece and Rome. Cayce said she was proficient in what was " . . . known as carrying the apple, or the running in what is called now the relay, or the governing of same" (934-1, T22).

In that lifetime, Cayce described T.J.'s mother as " . . . fleet of foot, of mind, of body; and many there were that held the entity in a position much of worshipfulness because of the abilities during the experience" (934-1, T24).

Born Burlynn Latham on January 2, 1910, in Portsmouth, Ohio, T.J.'s mother also was interested in athletics in this life. Like Boyd, her athletic abilities were strong during her years at Portsmouth High School, with her 1928 yearbook citing her involvement with track and basketball among her many interests.

Cayce gave a detailed accounting of Burlynn's karmic journey in previous lives. She had several interesting lifetimes in which Cayce and T.J. were present. She was one of the Atlanteans who came to Egypt, so since T.J. helped establish this group, they may well have known each other then. Cayce said she:

> . . . came into the Egyptian experience when there were the turmoils and strifes among the natives and the Priest and the King that was set as the ruler.

Then the entity joined with many of the rebellious forces that arose, and was known as being among those who continued to cause turmoils among various groups that were attempting to be quieted by the one or the other groups.

With the reestablishing of the Priest, though, in the Egyptian experience - when there was the return from the Libyan land, the entity then joined rather with those who made for the correlating and the material application of the tenets and experiences that were set in the peoples; especially as to the hospitalizations of those activities, and as to the GROUPS making practical application (934-1, T29–31).

It was in this lifetime that Burlynn developed her interest in nursing, but it also was this lifetime in which her self-indulgences arose.

Another fascinating lifetime for Burlynn was during the reign of Charles the Second while he was in exile. Then a male named Dubuquer, she was close to Charles and instrumental in bringing him back to the English throne. Afterward, their relationship floundered and Dubuquer became a soldier of fortune, traveling the world.

Of all her past lives, it is the one in which Burlynn was at Fort Dearborn that is most intriguing because it was there she was involved with the soul of Cayce, known then as Bainbridge. Burlynn—called Bergher at the time—was, in Cayce's words: "one of the girls" (934-1, T12) that Bainbridge courted and this, no doubt, set up his fondness for her in this lifetime. She had some karmic gains in the latter part of that life as a teacher and as being " . . . among the first of those that attempted to establish in that new land, in and about what is now Cincinnati, the form of economics for the new peoples that came to the land" (934-1, T14).

This lifetime explains where her karmic tug to Ohio originated—a tug shared by the soul of her son, who, according to Cayce, helped to establish the Mound Builders in the northern portions of Ohio after the fall of Atlantis.

Both Boyd and Burlynn had quite the karmic pedigree and were poised to come back as a powerhouse couple whose son would make a great impact on the world. So, what happened to this couple—and to the soul family attached to them—that put them on an alternate course?

The fact that Boyd was more interested in marrying his high school sweetheart than Burlynn, who had already been married, was the first red flag that this couple was ill fated. Yet despite Boyd's misgivings, the two married on September 17, 1934. Right from the start the couple had problems. Burlynn became pregnant immediately and went back to Ohio where she had an abortion. She later confided to Gladys that the baby had been a girl. T.J.'s speculation that the last thing his parents wanted was a baby could not have been truer.

The Davises' already crumbling marriage may have been Burlynn's motivation in aborting her first baby. Within months of their marriage, she had filed for divorce. It was a letter from Gladys that ultimately caused her to change her mind, but the seeds were planted for the early onset of the love-hate relationship she and Boyd would experience the rest of their lives.

By October, Boyd was concerned that Burlynn might be pregnant again. Writing from Ft. Myers, Florida, he asked Edgar Cayce for a reading for her that would outline what needed to be done for a healthy, normal child.

Cayce did as Boyd requested, giving a reading on Burlynn on November 22, 1935, while he was at the Warshawsky home in Detroit, Michigan. Gladys was present at that reading in which Cayce confirmed the pregnancy and discussed Burlynn's state of mind.

> Conception has taken place. There needs, then, be those precautions; not only *mentally* and physically for the body *itself* but as to the *attitude* and the manner of the associations of those *about* the body.

> Under the existent conditions, both physically *and* mentally, a great deal of anxiety on the part of the body, [934], naturally exists.

And these fears, these anxieties, must be met in *patience*; and not in any manner that tends to excite the general nervous reaction that is so natural as the developments in the existent conditions form or make their *normal* process (934-3, T3–5).

In this reading, he also cautioned both Boyd and Burlynn about the responsibility that was before them, given the serious work that lay ahead of their unborn child.

For, as you each - now - are responsible for that channel through which a soul may manifest in materiality; then in love, in faith, in hope, in prayer, *prepare* that channel that *that* soul - that may be drawn through those activities that are in preparation - may be as one that may be a blessing to not only those upon whom the body is dependent, but through that it may give of itself in and as a channel of hope, of blessings, to others (934-3, T11).

The last part of this reading gave the parents-to-be a simple but powerful message:

Stay close together! knowing that this is an

equal expression of each. And - *together* - present yourselves before the Lord! (934-3, T18).

Gladys had sat through countless readings, but this one, in particular, really moved her. She shared her emotional reaction with Burlynn in a letter dated December 18, 1935, telling her that reading was the most beautiful one she had ever heard. It made her want to be close to the couple to help in any way she could, even if only to send out loving thoughts for the baby. Gladys hoped Burlynn was rejoicing over the prospect of giving birth to a soul who had the potential of doing so much for the world.

"I feel that something so beautiful and so precious is going to happen that none of us can ever, ever, give expression fully of our thanks to the Father for allowing such a miracle," she wrote. "I wish you could have listened at the reading being given. But you will have just as great a thrill one of these days when you hear its Life Reading, and find out what you've attracted—but you'll already know that it's the sweetest, darlingest baby in the world!"

Anticipating the arrival of this very beloved soul, Edgar Cayce did all he could to keep the couple together. Even before T.J.'s birth, he took on the role of counselor, trying to impress on Boyd and Burlynn the magnitude of their responsibility to the incoming soul.

In a December 9, 1935, letter to them both, Cayce

advised that the couple "take a hold on things now," but his advice was to no avail. That same month, Boyd was arrested for having a slot machine at his business, the Tamiami Lunch Stand. A new city ordinance had banned slot machines within the city limits, and Boyd's lunch stand was four blocks inside those limits. Boyd argued that he did not know the distributing agent who left the machine at his place, but when the agent was arrested, Boyd admitted knowing who he was. The agent's defense was that he thought Boyd's lunch stand was outside the city limits. The newspaper reports said that Burlynn, described as "youthful and pretty," arrived at the police station shortly after Boyd had been jailed and called the arrest an outrage. He was released on a $100 recognizance bond. His December 30, 1935, letter to Edgar described their desperation, saying they had no money to pay their bills, much less hold on to the business. He asked Cayce for a reading to give them advice on what to do.

Cayce was sympathetic. In some ways, he felt responsible for Boyd and Burlynn's situation, as he had given Boyd a reading in August 1935 advising him to open the business in Ft. Myers. At first, it seemed like a success, as Boyd reported in mid-November that everything was "getting better all the time" but by Christmas, he was in trouble again. Nonetheless, Cayce encouraged Boyd to hold fast. Writing to him on January 6, 1936, Cayce not only expressed his concern for the young couple, but for the soul that was on the way. He believed things would work out and encouraged them to stay together.

Cayce said he would be glad to do another reading, but explained to Boyd that the outcome of a reading depended on the decisions made by the reading's recipient. While this advice applied to all who received a Cayce reading, it eerily forewarned what would happen to T.J. if his parents did not follow Cayce's advice. Cayce wrote:

> And we have had the experience of the readings through the last thirty-five years. I know, from the good that has been brought into the experience of individuals, the work is worthwhile. I can't be fooled that long, and I couldn't fool the thousands of people that claim and testify that it has been valuable to them. Now *you* make it valuable in your life! The reading may tell you the things to do for your best development, materially, mentally, spiritually; it may give you the knowledge, but the *doing* is up to *you*!

Cayce realized none of this was any of his business and that he was coming across "like a Dutch uncle" but felt that tough love was exactly what Boyd needed.

For her part, Burlynn tried to focus on whatever silver lining she could find in their otherwise gloomy predicament. Acknowledging her pregnancy as "something so worthwhile to live for now" she admitted to Edgar that "it's going to take a lot of self-sacrifice and that's something neither of us are very well versed in but with an inspiration such as we have, it won't be hard."

While she complained about life in Florida and their run-in with the law, she nonetheless called it, "a great lesson in perseverance and I believe that was the big reason the reading sent us here . . . I really believe this experience will do us good. Anyone can be cheerful around a big cozy fire with a lot of life's special comforts but it takes a few hardships to make 'men' of us, don't you think?"

Boyd did not want Cayce to blame himself for the trouble he was in and said so in his follow-up letter of January 9, but added that he had some very real issues to deal with, not the least of which was "to get something to eat and a place to sleep." They already had been given notice to vacate the premises and were trying to stay together, but Burlynn felt her husband would have a better chance of gaining employment if they moved to Ohio where they could live with her mother with minimum expense.

Boyd didn't want Cayce to believe he was running away, but added he felt that he had already stayed too long. He told Cayce he didn't know why the readings sent him to Florida, but he was sure it was for some purpose other than making a living. It might have been to get him out of that kind of work altogether. Whatever its meaning, his concern was that Burlynn have nutritious food and sufficient rest and that her mother's place was where she could have both.

Cayce wrote back immediately and agreed it would be best if the couple moved to Portsmouth, but again stressed the importance that they stay together. "Keep hold of yourself, and whatever comes—don't let it separate you two at this time. *Stay with it*! Because Burlynn needs you, as you need her, at this time as you never have before in your life."

Within a week, Boyd sold his half-interest in the business and by January 17 was writing to Cayce from Ohio, assuring him that Burlynn seemed happier.

In March, Cayce did another reading for Boyd in which he prepared him for T.J.'s arrival, only a few months away. But judging from the questions Boyd posed for the reading, he was more interested in information concerning his business interests. All his questions revolved around the dog track, his investment in a concession stand, potential business partnerships, and how he was going to manage to keep his car. When he asked whether a sandwich stand on the corner of 14th Street and Atlantic Avenue would be profitable for him that summer, Cayce's Source suggested he move a block down to 15th Street, as the 14th Street location was not very desirable. Boyd learned this prediction was true the hard way after he opened a stand at the corner of 14th and Atlantic. It was at this location that Gladys said he began to turn more and more to drinking beer to drown his troubles.

One gets a very clear sense of frustration, even in the readings, where Boyd is concerned. When he asks:

"How can I meet the payments that are due?" the answer is blunt, telling Boyd to " . . . get out and work!" (391-16, T21).

Sometime between that reading in March and T.J.'s birth in June, the couple returned to Virginia. Gladys's mother had come to the Beach to help Burlynn, but ended up having a stroke a few weeks before T.J. was born.

According to what T.J. remembered Edgar telling him, Cayce knew T.J. would be born on June 21, 1936, which was the summer solstice and the longest day of the year. Ironically, it also was Father's Day. T.J. later learned that a few days before he was born, Edgar told Gladys that his birth would be a little tricky but that she shouldn't worry about it and the baby would be okay. T.J. credits that assurance with why Gladys was so calm and collected, knowing instinctively what to do after he was born.

After spending nine months in his mother's womb, nurtured by almost nothing but alcohol, T.J. speculated that his soul must have questioned his decision to come into the world through Boyd and Burlynn. "You might say I was loaded the whole time and I hadn't even been born yet," he surmised. "I can just visualize myself in the womb saying, 'Oh God, another day.' I would check the calendar, so to speak, and give myself a pep talk about hanging in there."

This lackluster beginning wasn't what he had in mind. T.J. assumed, since he had had several lofty past lives, that he'd have an easy time slipping into this life, but it didn't work out like that. It wasn't as if he hadn't been forewarned. He believed that somehow Edgar conveyed the news directly to his soul that he'd have a little trouble getting here this time. But T.J. was confident all would work out in the end and he'd make it to the Cayce household, knowing as he did that their lives intermingled. "I always saw our incarnations as being part of one large club or family, so I knew exactly where I belonged," he said. "For now, I just had to go with the flow."

Virginia Beach was a very small town in 1936, with no hospital and only one physician, Dr. Waller Taylor, who delivered every baby at home. Taylor knew about Burlynn's drinking and according to T.J., expressed concern to Gladys about the baby's well-being throughout her pregnancy.

By the time T.J. was born at home at 2:45 p.m., he was near death. "I definitely looked weird," he said. "My skin was almost like wood. Dr. Taylor told my parents that my body was drying up. He said I'd probably be dead in three days and they should plan for my funeral. Meanwhile, there was Mr. Cayce, fully cognizant of my condition long before anyone told him. He calmly asked Gladys to see if my parents would agree to let me stay with him. He said he would fix me up and I'd be just fine."

So according to T.J., Gladys went to her brother's house to talk to him about taking the as-yet-unnamed baby boy to the Cayces. T.J. said that even though he was only a few days old, his parents had already resumed their heavy drinking and gambling. When Gladys asked about taking him to the Cayce home,

Although taken years later, this is a photo of T.J. with his cousin Ann in front of the house where he was born in Oceana. (ECF#1387)

T.J. said his mother really didn't care and his dad actually thought it was a good idea. "After all," he said. "Everybody thought I'd be dead in a few days anyway, so they just shuffled me off to the man of miracles."

T.J. said Gladys brought him to Edgar, who gave him a quick reading, telling Gladys, "Don't worry. Put him on Carnation milk and he'll be okay in the morning." She did—and he was.

For Gladys, having T.J. in her care brought out

her maternal instincts. On the day he was born, a notation was made attached to reading (288-29, R2): "Her nephew [1208] was born, satisfying the longing for a son of her own."

T.J. credits Edgar Cayce for coming up with his name. "When my parents were told I wouldn't last more than a few days, they didn't bother to give me a name so for the first three days of my life, I was nameless," he said.

Dr. Taylor came to give the baby a checkup at the Cayce house and brought a blank birth certificate with him. It listed both of his parents as twenty-five years of age, describing his father as a merchant and his mother as a housewife. T.J. said Dr. Taylor told Edgar that the baby needed a name and asked him what they were going to call him. Without hesitation, Edgar said, "Call him Thomas Jefferson."

"I can still feel that moment," T.J. said. "I know it's probably my imagination, but I can see him and Gladys smiling to themselves and hearing a little drumroll in the background when he announced, 'Call him Thomas Jefferson.'"

T.J. admits he is not certain whether Edgar named him Thomas Jefferson after Cayce's grandfather, Thomas Jefferson Cayce, or after our third president, but his sense is that it was the latter. "He knew who I had been in a previous lifetime, so it would make sense that he'd give me that name. In any case, I wasn't so thrilled about having that name, realizing what it would cost me later, but Thomas Jefferson Davis it was."

T.J. said as he grew older, he and Edgar had more serious conversations about how they came to live together.

"Once Mr. Cayce asked me if I remembered anything about preparing to be born and finding him," T.J. recalled. "I said, 'Of course. We all had to get here somehow.' When I said 'we' I meant all members of Mr. Cayce's soul family. For me it was like catching the Red Eye—getting on a plane that was leaving very late and having to fly through the darkness, but eventually landing in the light. I felt as though I had been prepped for the long and difficult journey by a guardian angel. I was reassured everything would be all right in that I'd find Mr. Cayce and I would be just fine. That was a comfort, for during my mother's entire pregnancy, I understood why I was there and I knew once I was born, Mr. Cayce would take care of me. I remember we talked about this with that matter-of-fact air that was the hallmark of our conversations. 'You did a good job, T.J.,' Mr. Cayce said. 'So here we are together—fishing.'"

Looking back over his life, T.J. said he could not help but be astounded at how Edgar accurately depicted what lay ahead for that helpless two-day-old baby boy who was the focus of so much attention that June day in 1936.

Chapter Two
Setting the Stage: T.J.'s Life Reading

On June 23, 1936, at 11:30 a.m., Edgar gave what would be T.J.'s first and only life reading. Cayce intended to provide T.J. with a second life reading when he turned thirteen, but Edgar's premature death prevented that pivotal reading from ever happening.

A review of T.J.'s life reading is essential before getting into the Davis or Cayce family dynamic, as Cayce gave very specific instructions as to the upbringing of this baby boy, now referred to as #1208. Here, as in his subsequent health readings, Edgar was adamant that T.J. receive the correct guidance and training in his formative years in order that he learn to use all of the positive karmic gifts that he earned in previous lifetimes. For Cayce it wasn't so much who T.J. had been, but who he could become.

While the four past lives Edgar gave T.J. at this reading will be discussed in greater detail in chapter 14, there were other key points that Cayce's Source made about young T.J. that were prophetic. Here is the text of that reading, with intermittent comments about certain aspects of Cayce's predictions and warnings that came to pass.

TEXT OF READING 1208-1 M 2 DAYS
(Christian Background)
This psychic reading given by Edgar Cayce at his home on Arctic Crescent, Virginia Beach, Va., this 23rd day of June, 1936, in accordance with request made by the parents - Mr. [391] and Mrs. [934], Active Members of the Ass'n for Research & Enlightenment, Inc.

PRESENT
Edgar cayce; Gertrude Cayce, Conductor; Gladys Davis, Steno. Mr. [391], Thomas House and Hugh Lynn Cayce.

READING
Born June 21, 1936, at 2:45 P.M., Sunday (Father's Day), at the home of his parents, Virginia Beach, Virginia. Time of Reading 11:30 to 12:00 A.M. Eastern Standard Time. ..., Va. (Life Reading Suggestion)

1. EC: [[1208] named.]

2. Yes, we have the entitiy here, those relations with the universe and universal forces, that are recorded in the experiences of this entity through the earth's plane as well as those environs in the activities about the earth. Its earthly experience as related to the activities of the entity to many, especially in the land of the nativity and especially at this particular season would become most astounding. Yet if there are the developments through the environs, it may be seen that *this* entity - [1208] - may become more important in the affairs of the *world* than this entity in its previous experience has been to America - Thomas Jefferson.

3. In giving the experiences of the entity, and those influences that will bear upon the development of the etity, we find that these - for this entity in the present - have some peculiar or unusual turns.

In paragraphs four and six, Edgar was clear about what needed to be done regarding T.J.'s upbringing, with warnings about what would happen if those instructions were not heeded.

4. From the astrological aspects we find the entity almost *exactly* upon the cusps. Hence we will find two influences, and the entity of needing, requiring, a consideration by those making the choice of environs for the entity during the early portion of its developments.

5. That there are then responsibilities, this becomes apparent. For there has been into this keeping, in these beginnings, entrusted in this experience an entity that may mean as much to the world as the entity meant to, means to, America.

6. Make then for those influences that there may be not the pampering, yet a development wherein there may be the *opportunities* for the *entity's own* development. Yet choices of that as is to be the entity's ideal will depend upon the manner in which corrections are made, the manner in which moral fortitude is manifested, the manner in which the general impressions are made upon the developing mind of this entity.

7. Coming under those influences of

Gemini and Scorpio, as are indicated, there will be tendencies for weaknesses in the early developing; requiring that those caring for the body be mindful as to the digestive forces and that there is kept an equal balance - else there may come, of course, those experiences of an early change in the activity, or in the sojourn. In these then the proper precautions should be taken, that there are the proper relationships and that there is the proper balance kept between those things that produce acid and those that keep an alkalin balance in the digestive forces of the body. [See 1208-2 through 1208-5, etc.]

8. Save from these, as we find, if these precautions are kept, little experience of anxiety may be felt as respecting the activities in the conditions throughout the entity's experience.

9. Hence if these precautions are taken and the care of the body is made in this direction during the first year and six months, the entity would almost grow and care for itself.

Cayce added that T.J.'s intellect needed to be

properly directed.

> 10. As has been indicated through the periods, this influence in Mercury will make for a high *mental* development. With the experience as has been indicated this must be directed. For if these tendencies are turned from the right *mental* attitudes *as* to choices, these may be as detrimental as they are beneficial. For the entity will be, as it has been, an extremist - in *all* of its associations. And what it wants it will *want now!* In these respects then there will be needed the proper precautions as to the reasoning with the entity. For, as will be the natural nature, it will be an arguer from the beginnings - and make for demands such that there will have to be a reason, and this expressed in no uncertain terms in the entity's development.

As if to confirm Cayce's prediction that T.J. would be "an arguer from the beginnings," in March 1947, Gladys included a notation in his reading about an argument he had with his cousin:

> Miss [288] wrote: "I heard [1208] and [1635] arguing about their respective birthdates in June. [1635] said:

'[1208], you will not be 12 years on your next birthday!'

"[1208]: 'Well, how do you suppose I get to go to all the Scout Meetings then?'

"[1635]: I don't know, but you're just 2 yrs. older than I am, and I'll only be 9 on my birthday.'

"[1208] (Thinking a minute): 'Yes, [1635], but I saw my birth certificate, and I was born a year before I was supposed to be.'"

11. From Jupiter, which we find as the ruling influence, then, there comes the influence wherein the entity will make for friendships in *every* association, of all characters. Here again there must be not the associations without a reason, but a reasoning with the entity for its choice of associations. For, as the entity in its relationships must belong as it were to the *world,* it will regard all peoples alike. For those influences and activities will be the greater influence, if those directions are made in the experiences of its development as to its proper relationships and choices as to its associations.

T.J.'s reading further stated that he would make friends with people from every walk of life, and that certainly turned out to be true considering the worldwide travels that awaited him.

> 12. For the high and the low, those of fame and those of defame, will be *as one* to the entity without reason - unless guided aright.

> 13. The influences of Mercury as combined *with* those in Venus make for the natural tendency for what may be termed a piddler; that is, in *everything* will the entity in part excel, whether this be in music - as a fiddler - or whether as one that would make for new applications of the *old* conditions in the affairs of individuals. A natural arguer; then a natural orator also.

T.J. said he did not understand nor believe reference to his being a "natural orator" until he started giving talks about his years with Mr. Cayce to the A.R.E. group in Charlottesville. "Although I was nervous at first, when I relaxed it did come quite naturally and everyone commented favorably about my skills as a storyteller," he said.

> 14. And he will be able to argue most everyone down, unless those tendencies are directed aright.

T.J. admits he was an arguer when he was younger, but that he eventually out grew it.

> 15. A natural scribe, as is indicated from the very *love* of *experiences* through the entire experience of the entity in this sojourn. Hence by some it will be termed a meddler; for it will be into everything - as a curiosity. Nothing will be strange to the entity, but - to know *why* it works!

"In terms of nothing being strange to me, I can say I honestly have never looked at anything with astonishment or awe because after living with Mr. Cayce, I knew at an early age that anything was possible," T.J. said. "But he was right about my desire to know why things work the way they do—what forces are in play to enable events to happen, relationships to begin and end, the very reason for it all."

> 16. As to the appearances in the earth and those that influence the entity in the present - if there are the activities directed or guided as has been indicated in its sojourn in the early portion, or the formative years, in the choice of the entity:

> 17. Before this, as given, the entity lived in the earth during those periods when

there were the turmoils in that known as
the Revolution, and in the activities of the
Colonists.

18. The entity then, as Thomas Jefferson,
made these contributions to the activities
of the people - that are well known, or may
be had through the many references that
may be drawn upon by those seeking to
know. [Yrs. 1743-1826]

19. But rather seek to know the *basic
forces* that *directed* same. For the inventive
genius that *prompted* the activities of the
entity then, the curious nature that made
for the many oppositions that arose in
the experience, are those things that are
indicated in the two natures that apparently
will be in the developing period of the
entity's activities.

20. Hence in the application of same, not
because of *"he was"* but because these
may be *used*, there should be the correct
guidance and training in his formative
years. For as a great landowner will the
entity be if it reaches the years of its
majority.

While T.J. doesn't consider himself a great landowner by historic standards, he does own close to forty acres in Albermarle County, Virginia, and compared to other county residents, that is "great" indeed.

21. The experience before that we find was in those periods when there were the disturbances in or the establishing of that land now called France, when there wre the first of the separations through the Gallic Wars, through the activities that made for separation for the east or for the west portions of the Helvetic activities - the Romans and Britons and the Normans. [Yrs. 200-100 B.C.?]

22. The entity then was among those that made for the establishing or the setting of this apart in those periods of the experience, in the name then Donquiellen.

23. In the experience the entity gained and lost. Gained, and through those activities brought into the influences of those peoples that which has remained much of the basic forces of that as a nation, that as a people, that has been as a *separate* influence in the affairs of the world throughout the periods since that establishment.

24. Hence we find in the application in the entity's experience in the present, those very influences for power - if they are not merely idealistic but purposeful, with the ideals of a union for an application - will bring not only material but the spiritual benefits in those activities of the earth.

25. For the entity from those very things may become that one who may make of the world as *one* nation, and those of other lands as but states in *one* grand kingdom.

26. Before that we find the entity was in that land during those periods when there were the activities that made for the rise and fall of many lands, in the Grecian, the Persian, all of the eastern lands; when *that* entity now known as Alexander the Great made for the conquering forces of the earth - the depleting that there might bring to self the exaltations [356-323 B.C.] [See 3976-4 on 2/11/27.]

27. *Here* the entity lost. For these will become in the experience of the entity those influences that might makes for right, or power making for indulgences. And if

these are not conquered in the experiences as the principles that are set in its earthly experience, these may run as wild in the very activities of the entity - even as then.

28. Before that we find the entity was in the land now known as the Atlantean, when there were the disturbances upon which those divisions arose.

29. The entity then took the part of those who later became the heads of those that warred against those of the Law of One, and then in the name of Sululon - as would be termed in the present.

30. In those experiences that entity made for destructive froces in the early experiences, yet with those activities that brought about the union in body with one of the daughters of the Law of One, the entity then become to each group as one set apart. For the teachers of the Law of One were afraid of the ability, while those that were of the sons of Belial were afraid of the entity becoming what would be termed in the present as a traitor.

31. Hence throughout those periods the

entity became then *that one* that led the first establishing of the activity in the varied lands that came to be known as later the Mayan, the Yucatan, the Inca, the Peruvian - and *later* the Mound Builders in the northern portions of the entity's present sojourn. [Ohio?]

32. Not that the entity remained there, but established those activities which has become a part of the entity by those divisions.

33. Hence we find in these three expeditions or experiences, while the principles are the same, the expressions of same, the expressions of same are in varying *manners* of manifestation, coming from the one *mental* or *physical being's* mind - for a development. Or as called by many, as may be in the present, a meddler with things that to many are dangerous.

34. As to the abilities then of the entity in the present, that to which it may attain and how: These become as problematicals in those that may be about, those that may have to do with, its early developments. But *rule* rather than be ruled, for the entity

will tend to rule all about same.

35. When the entity has passed its thirteenth year, begin again.

36. We are through for the present.

Much of what Cayce said in the life reading was confirmed three years later in an astrological reading given by Lillian Frieda Frey. In a letter to Gladys she wrote:

> According to the time you gave me, your nephew, Thomas, has Scorpio rising and in his case its ruler is in the 8th house causing him to have a tendency to research on other planes. He will not be psychic as Mr. Cayce is but will he highly intellectual and intuitive; his Sun, Mars, Mercury, Venus being in the 8th house also.
>
> There is a tendency to be self-willed and an effort should be made to train it into constructive channels.
>
> His Moon and Pluto are conjunct in the 9th house, which usually indicates some long journies.
>
> Jupiter is in his own house in Sagittarius

and regardless of how things might go in a financial way he should always have enough to get by.

This was the auspicious start of T.J.'s life with his future spread out like a magnificent buffet table of possibilities. Everyone knew the reading well—not only those who were present that day, but scores of other individuals who heard that this extraordinary soul was now in the care of the Davis and Cayce families. But no one knew that reading better than T.J., as Gladys read it to him nightly as one would a bedtime story.

So now the stage is set. The players have read the script. All they needed to do was to perform their part until he came of age and could continue the course to fulfill his destiny.

Chapter Three

1937–1938: An Unsteady Start

Burlynn with T.J., circa 1938–39. (ECF#1006)

While T.J. may have believed that his father agreed to allow his Aunt Gladys to raise him as her own from birth, the records show that when he was a month old, he was still living with his mother. That does not negate Cayce's influence on the baby. Burlynn's reliance on Cayce for guidance is apparent in her countless requests for health readings, starting when T.J. was five days old.

One incident, in particular, stands out and sets the tone for what would become a familiar family pattern in T.J.'s life. When asked in a reading given on June 26, 1936, if there was any special food his mother should avoid, Cayce eluded to the family quarrels—not just certain foods—that the baby needed to avoid: "As has been indicated, *fats* are the most detrimental to all infants in this developing stage. And *anger*! Keep from *anger*!" (1208-2, T11).

T.J. was a month old when Gladys reported that Burlynn got mad at Boyd, went out, drank beer, came back, and then nursed her son. T.J. had problems with his stomach from the moment he was born, but this only made it worse. He said he could imagine Edgar and his parents engaged in an endless struggle for control over his welfare.

"My mother would do something stupid, like nursing me after she had been drinking, and then she would run to Mr. Cayce and ask for a remedy," he commented.

This particular time, however, T.J.'s stomach became upset and a rash spread over his body. Dr. Taylor kept recommending the same milk formula, which was a combination of Burlynn's milk and cow's milk. The baby's skin got so bad that it was peeling off in flakes, until Burlynn finally decided it was time to seek an alternative treatment. Writing to Cayce, Burlynn pleaded for a reading.

That same day Cayce gave the reading, acknowledging that the baby's health was in jeopardy. But even with the reading, there was doubt that he'd live. Cayce changed T.J.'s formula back to Carnation milk and added castoria in small doses, plus yellow saffron in his water. He said the baby's " . . . internal system is in much *worse* condition even than that indicated in the skin or on the body and the mouth and neck" (1208-3, T7).

Cayce suggested using equal portions of camphorated oil with olive oil as an ointment for the rash and then adamantly warned not to use anything other than Carnation milk. "Do not *change* from one to another" (1208-3, T10) seemed to rebuke Dr. Taylor's advice. He also told Burlynn to stop nursing, saying when she did, it caused " . . . more of the infectious forces for the whole system" (1208-3, T20).

Once Burlynn began to follow Cayce's instructions, T.J.'s condition improved. Gladys noted that two hours after T.J. was given the new formula he went to sleep and rested for the first time since the condition started.

"He did it again," T.J. said. "He saved my life."

As precarious as T.J.'s physical condition was at that time, Burlynn was considering leaving Virginia Beach with him, going so far as to ask Cayce for permission to do so. Cayce answered that T.J., "Will have to be in much better fix than he is in the present" (1208-3, T21) before she could leave, adding that even after his condition improved, it was a choice only she could make. However, he gave her fair warning. "*First* there must be the consideration of the baby, if it would be kept alive" (1208-3, T22).

Several days later, Cayce followed up with another health reading, indicating that while T.J.'s condition was still serious, there were signs of improvement. This is the first time Cayce recommended the addition of a drop of glyco-thymoline be given before each nursing. The use of glyco-thymoline as an internal antiseptic of an alkaline nature is recommended in numerous health readings. Interesting to note that T.J. has used glyco-thymoline ever since, crediting it with his overall excellent health as an adult.

When reviewing T.J.'s health readings, Cayce's Source implored Burlynn to be more patient and discerning in the care of her child. For instance, in the follow-up reading two weeks later, Cayce said that although there was slight improvement, the baby's condition was still very serious. When it was asked why the baby stiffened his spine as if he were in pain, Cayce's Source said it was a natural reaction to what he had been subjected to and then added that it was a good spine and that Burlynn should " . . . give it a chance for goodness' sakes!" (1208-4, T13).

When pressed further about adding tea to T.J.'s

diet, Cayce's Source answered:

> Not until, as has been indicated! It may be one day, it may be a week—but it's the necessity of alleviating those disturbances internally. If you don't, we will have the inflammation continually pouring out through the respiratory system, of the infectious forces, see? This is left off until such time as has been indicated! Use some judgement and some discretion; if you don't, you'll make it much worse (1208-4, T15).

In 1208-5, T14, Burlynn asks: "Of what should those in charge be most precautious from now on?" To which Cayce's Source answered, "As has been *given*! Be *consistent*!"

In the next reading, Cayce's Source was asked again if the milk formula should be changed. He responded, "*Do not* change! We didn't change it, did we?" (1208-6, T12).

By mid-August T.J.'s condition had improved, but Gladys began to see how invaluable the readings would be in keeping T.J. alive. In a letter dated August 12, 1936, Gladys acknowledged the link between T.J.'s reading and his current condition.

Little [1208] didn't take long in fulfilling

his reading (1208-1); he has had an awful time with this stomach... If we hadn't gotten the readings on him, too, he wouldn't have lived through it...Now he is, we believe, out of danger and is getting fat. He just smiles and coos all the time...although not 2 months old he can raise himself on his little hands (lying on his stomach) and look up at the light. He just loves every tiny crack of light and all the time he was broken out we had to keep him in a dark room.

Being part of the Cayce household at such a young age, and considering all T.J. went through to reach Mr. Cayce, is it no wonder that he had a fascination for the light!

T.J. may have been staying with Burlynn and her mother when the next health crisis developed. At that time, Gladys was working out of the Cayce home and taking care of T.J. only part of the time. Perhaps it was the duress of this unstable situation that caused Gladys to suffer a skin condition much like his. She admitted she was worn out from nursing him. She thought the skin flare-up was more from worry than anything else, adding she got immediate relief by applying the Atomidine, one of Cayce's remedies.

Within a day or two later, Burlynn and T.J. were gone. It must have been a shock to Gladys that they took off so abruptly, as acknowledged by Burlynn in a letter to her sister-in-law on August 18, in which she wrote: "You probably wonder what has happened to T.J. and me and a good bit has since we left you all."

Burlynn said she and the baby got as far as Farmville, but by then she was exhausted and began to get nervous. T.J. was crying for his bottle and she couldn't get his milk fixed. "It really seemed to terrify me and all at once I started to cry and laugh, then when I got that stopped I got numb all over just like I did that nite when you and your mother took care of me," she continued.

"The conductor got a man he knew to take me to the Virginian Hotel in Lynchburg but I was pretty sick all nite and at 5 o'clock Friday morning they took me to Memorial Hospital in Lynchburg. The superintendent, a Miss Vaupelt, took me in to her room and took care of the baby and me herself. I guess it's about the sickest I have ever been but I believe I'll be all rite [right] now that I'm home.

"T.J. was pretty sick, too, but he has plenty of pluck, bless his little old heart. He stayed right alongside of me and when we finally arrived here, my sister had a baby specialist come and they straightened him out, gave him an enema, a bath, a good dinner and put him to bed. He slept like a little log and has been gaining ever since. All the crust came off his head and he's looking so good."

Burlynn told Gladys that she and her mother would be back in Virginia Beach after Labor Day and would get a place to live at the Beachome Apartments on

28th and Atlantic. Her mother agreed to pay their rent, and Burlynn felt confident she could manage their expenses if she could find work.

"Tell Mrs. Cayce I'll come back with her baby if she'll forgive me for wanting my Fuller Broom back," she wrote. She then added, "I'd rather you wouldn't mention to Boyd about my coming back."

A week later, on August 25, 1936, Gladys wrote that T.J.'s parents had separated. "It is surprising that a soul – such a soul – would choose that environment; still, as the rdg. (1208-1) says, there are two sides to him and he can be a power either way."

By the end of August, Burlynn was having some misgivings about returning with her mother. She acknowledged she loved her mother, but the two didn't get along and now was the time for her to try and live alone. She told Gladys she and T.J. would be arriving in Norfolk the day after Labor Day and asked her to look into the winter rates at the Beachome Apartments.

T.J. and Burlynn were in Virginia Beach until November when they returned to Portsmouth, but there is no record of what precipitated this decision. Boyd continued to be hopeful they would reconcile although he told Edgar he had been planning to go to South America. However, Boyd kept dreaming of T.J. and what he would be like later as he grew up, so he felt forced to go to Ohio and get them. Burlynn returned and the family was united once again.

Gladys, Edgar, Gertrude, and T.J., August 1937. (ECF#0960)

The couple's happiness was short-lived. Following her return with T.J. to Virginia Beach, Burlynn was diagnosed with a severe uterine infection for which she was briefly hospitalized and soon thereafter underwent a partial hysterectomy.

By the time T.J. was six months old, people who knew of him began to show a greater interest in his life, treating him as if he were royalty. Even at this young age, he enjoyed getting attention. Gladys, ever the proud aunt, acted almost like his manager, gleeful about sharing his progress.

Boyd continued to pursue self-employment, opening the Bama Boys Refreshment Stand, which soon failed. Once again facing legal problems due to not filing an income tax report for the business, Boyd wrote to the Department of Taxation to say the business partnership had been dissolved, as the stand was open only ten weeks in the summer and did not take in enough to justify an income tax report. Nonetheless, he opened a second Bama

Boys Refreshment Stand, called Bama Boys #2, on 26th Street, but within a year the ABC license for this business was suspended.

T.J.'s health issues continued through the summer. On August 12, 1937, just two months after his first birthday, Cayce gave another reading for him that primarily focused on health issues, but then changed tone and gave his parents yet another warning about his upbringing.

> In the care of the mental and the spiritual atmosphere of the body – watch the developments, the tendencies. Be positive but not severe with the mental forces and influences of the body; this is much preferable to that of severity. Do not break the will, but rather guide same in the constructive suggestions as to the activities of the body in every way and manner. These kept, as we find we will have a developing body, mentally and physically near to normal (1208-8, T8–9).

Boyd and Burlynn were present at this reading, along with Gertrude Cayce and Gladys. It is not clear who asked which questions, but the advice about how to rear the child was brought up again.

(Q) Is there further information that can

be given the parents that will be helpful in training him during the next few years?

(A) These that have been given are the manners; positive but not making for such severeness as to break the will. Rather by precept *and example*; for remember, the example is well, as is the precept; but the example is much more effective to the body.

(Q) Is there a chance for [1208] making good as a baby actor in the movies? If so, how should we go about it?

(A) It isn't of the disposition or nature that it should be in such.

(Q) Please give us any other helpful information regarding the rearing of the child.

(A) This should be given as the development comes. For during these periods, or until after the eighteenth month, the precautions are most for the *physical* being. *Then* from the eighteenth month we may find more for the mental. And do not forget the spiritual atmosphere for the developing entity (1208-8, T15–17).

That winter, Boyd and Burlynn packed up T.J. and drove to Ohio for Christmas, but judging from the notation that Gladys made on January 3, 1938, they were negligent in their care of their eighteen-month-old son. He ran a high fever after being exposed to the cold and was being fed the wrong diet. His parents started him on the same treatment he had been on from an earlier reading and although the fever was somewhat allayed, he was still very sick.

Being back in Virginia Beach allowed Gladys and Edgar to keep a vigilant eye on him. Once again, Cayce gave the toddler a health reading and once again, T.J. made a miraculous recovery. Nonetheless, Boyd, Burlynn, and T.J. were in a seemingly unending cycle of serious health issues. When Boyd turned to Cayce for help with his own health issues, Cayce's Source cited his drinking as the cause of his worsening condition. This, coupled with the strain of not having steady employment, only added to the family's stress.

Watching this unfold was of deep concern to everyone as the Cayce readings called the couple to task once again for the decisions they were making and how it continued to impact T.J.

It was clear that Boyd was abusing his body and nothing would change unless he would change his behavior. "Do not *drink*, but *eat properly*! Do not *abuse* the body – either mentally *or* physically, but *most* of all by alcohol; and especially hops or the products of same, or even the carbonated waters are harmful for *this* body – and, of course, the *strong* drinks are more harmful!" (391-18, T23).

Chapter Four

1939–1940: "Expect Great Things .
. . Some Day"

T.J. (*center*) with two other Davis children tenants (no relation)

at the Beachome Apartments in 1938. (ECF#0987)

By January 1939, T.J. was living in Norfolk, but according to a letter Gladys wrote, she and the Cayces continued to see him once a week and occasionally on weekends. Cayce gave T.J. another health reading on January 30, 1939, but by February, the two-year-old came down with measles. The condition arose shortly after Burlynn once again had taken him back to Ohio to visit her family. She placed a frantic call to Edgar the morning of February 19, reporting T.J. had a high fever and was breaking out all over. She later realized her call had created alarm in the Cayce household and quickly followed up with a letter explaining her behavior, saying she was homesick and hadn't seen her family for over a year. Being faced with several unexpected situations —T.J. becoming ill the day after they arrived, her mother falling and breaking her leg, and T.J.'s condition steadily growing worse—Burlynn was "nearly frantic." The previous treatments Cayce had recommended weren't working this time.

"I'm sorry I had to worry you," Burlynn wrote to Edgar. "You've been so generous and kind and you love him so much, it makes it that much harder to ask you to give me more of your time. Someday I'm sure Thomas Jefferson will repay you. He's asked for you and Muddy Cayce and Gladys and wants to go to the Beachome. I don't know when I'll get home. Things aren't going so well in Norfolk either I understand. I think when I come home we'll move back to the Beachome where we can be near you. It seems we always get into trouble when we're too far away to run in and talk things over. Perhaps we can manage someway . . . Thank you, Mr. Cayce, from the bottom of my heart for giving us this reading. It gave me a great deal of encouragement just to hear your voice this morning."

Cayce gave the reading, and by early March 1939, Burlynn wrote that T.J. was feeling good and that she intended to come home within the week. She told Edgar that T.J. was homesick and talked about him all the time. "He pretends he's calling you up and he'll say, 'son's we visit Aunt Ruby, we'll be home Cakie,' and shake his head," she wrote.

The reference to Edgar as "Cakie" was something T.J. came up with on his own. "Even though Edgar Cayce was like a father to me, I knew I couldn't very well call him dad," he explained. "So what could I call him? I couldn't pronounce Edgar Cayce, so I just referred to him as Eddie Cay-kee!"

While Burlynn may have intended to return to Virginia Beach in early March, there are indications she remained in Ohio until June. A June 14, 1939, notation in Boyd's file stated that T.J. and Burlynn were expected from Portsmouth the next day. That may have been the case because he did spend his third birthday in Virginia Beach where Gladys reported he had a whole new set of health challenges. "Infected mosquito bites a couple of weeks ago, then new places started forming and wouldn't heal [Impetigo?]. Child cross, nervous, bad breath, bad color, restless at night on account of sores; no appetite. He has always put his finger in his ears and shook it as if it itched greatly; so the other night I put a drop of St. Jacob's Oil in each ear, - he woke up and cried several hours, - had to give him a little Aspirin water to get him to sleep again. The ear bled some and ran a dark red pus the next two days, - just one ear, - the other didn't seem to be affected. There's also a breaking out behind each ear, worse on the one affected internally. He must have gotten the infection from some children who had sores, with whom he played. He has taken approximately nineteen osteopathic treatments from Dr. Richardson, to absorb and drain adenoids; but his diet in the meantime has not been correct to keep up proper drainage. Still breathes heavily at night."

A month later, he again was dealing with inflamed adenoids. Cayce gave another health reading, urging the parents to follow the advice given in previous readings.

T.J.'s time at the Beach was short-lived. By September, he was separated again from Gladys and the Cayces—this time taken to Fort Worth, Texas, where Boyd had found a job earlier in the summer. The family moved into a duplex with a yard for T.J. to play in. There were two children his age living next door. Burlynn wrote that they played nicely together and that T.J. spent a lot of time outdoors. While Burlynn said she was crazy about Fort Worth, she again admitted she was homesick.

Meanwhile in Virginia Beach, Edgar Cayce was feeling the loss of T.J. In a September 8, 1939, letter, he wrote: "Miss Gladys's nephew has gone to Tex. to live - she has had him for last two months and makes it bad for her. Hope he keeps well - we are all crazy about him 'Thomas Jefferson.'"

A few weeks later, he followed up with a letter to Burlynn expressing the same sentiment. "Of course we miss you both, and miss that blessed little piece like we would our right arm." Referring to T.J.'s continuing respiratory issues, Edgar advised Burlynn to take T.J. to Dr. Charles F. Kenney to follow up on his condition in the hope of avoiding an operation to correct his adenoid and tonsil enlargement. Once T.J. completed several treatments, Edgar asked Burlynn to follow up and let him know how the boy was doing.

He ended by saying how quiet things were at the Beach and that it "looks very lonesome round the corner here….sure miss the boy—give him and Boyd our love, and let us hear from him as often as you can – *please*."

While Burlynn continued to write that she was dealing with occasional bouts of homesickness, she admitted that things in Fort Worth were good for the whole family. They had a nice place to live and T.J. looked better than he had in a long time, attributing his weight gain and better sleep to the climate. They attended services every Sunday, with T.J. in Sunday school, wowing everyone with his "amazing" singing voice. Burlynn seemed surprised at this burgeoning talent, saying, "I don't know how well he sings but I do know it's loud."

She was learning much about her son, including the connection everyone had to him. "It seems that we've all had something to do with Thomas Jefferson." In that same letter, she revealed T.J.'s merging talent as an artist, sending Gladys some of his drawings.

It seemed Edgar was always on the youngster's mind and the feeling was mutual. Edgar hoped T.J. would be home for Christmas, but that wasn't the case. Burlynn had teased that might happen by telling Lydia Schrader Gray, who had visited the family, that they'd be back for the holiday. In a letter to Edgar, Lydia wrote: "I'm wondering if you had little Thomas Jefferson - as a surprise gift - around Christmas time. His mother spoke of hoping to surprise Gladys & you all - by bringing him to Virginia Beach - while she and her husband attended some convention or Christmas party. He was so dear - and we enjoyed his lovely mother [Burlynn Latham Davis]."

After the holiday, Cayce answered a letter from Burlynn in which she discussed their plans to move yet again, this time to Alabama. He took the opportunity to express his disappointment about not seeing T.J., writing: " . . . couldn't you all make it to Va Beach when you were in Charlotte—the other week???? . . . Glad T.J. had such a fine time at Christmas and has enjoyed the little that we tried to get together—know he is the cutest smartest thing in the country—would give anything to have seen him—would have met you all in Charlotte had we known what day you would have been there. Tickled Gertrude what you said about his carrying the 'Uke.' . . . Had card from Mrs. Gray telling us about stopping to see you all. She said T.J. said that I was his Cakie—and that tickled me plenty."

Throughout the correspondence, it is clear that Cayce considered Boyd, and especially Burlynn, part of his soul's mission. In that same January 11 letter, he wrote: "Have missed you plenty—don't know how to figure it all out—but am still very sure—you must be one of my special missions in this old world especially after you told me something about your self. For there must not be any others. Give T.J. a big hug for me, and let us hear from you more often if you can possibly find time. You know there is no one we think more of—and all here most worship T.J. that you know."

By February 1940, their Texas sojourn officially was over. Boyd had been transferred to Montgomery, Alabama, but because they couldn't find a place to live, Burlynn and T.J. temporarily went back to Ohio.

By mid-March, the Davis family was getting settled at 518 Clayton Street in Montgomery, but already Burlynn was looking for a block of time when she would be alone. Despite the fact that he was much too young to go to kindergarten, being three months shy of his fourth birthday, Burlynn allowed the boy next door to take T.J. with him to school.

"I know he'll love it," she rationalized. "He's so crazy about drawing and writing and his association with other children will be good for him."

It is interesting that at this point in his life, many other souls were coming into contact with T.J. and commenting about his journey.

On April 27, 1940, [1196]—Cayce's friend from Alabama—wrote to Edgar after having visited Burlynn and T.J. in Montgomery. Edgar had encouraged his friend to visit T.J. with this enticement: "Friends of ours have recently moved to ... - in fact Miss [288]'s brother [391] and his wife [934] and boy [1208] - the boy a little fellow is the one that I wish you go see - think you and Mrs. [...] will find him worth knowing - see him then will tell you an interesting story that you will wish to follow up am sure. The address is ... Let me know about it won't you. And can we be of help - just call on me."

Upon receiving his friend's letter saying he had indeed visited T.J., Edgar shared the "interesting story" he promised. "Glad that you went to see our boy - the [1208] boy," wrote Edgar, "for we are all very very fond of him here, and expect great things for him some day - for this is the story. The information insists that he was Thomas Jefferson, in his last incarnation, and will have much to do with shaping the policies of this land again, - provided of course that he has the proper training in the formative years of his experience here, so every one that meets that child that has any conception of GOD'S plan with man has a real opportunity. Therefore was anxious that you know him, for am sure you wish to see and aid in seeing God's plan work in the affairs of man. Personally have had many experiences with the child that has convinced me, know they are not proofs for any one else but knowing what you are looking for is one thing and finding it is quite another that I know, but you with your abilities - can am sure with a little patience have much of the same experience as I. And hope you will take the time - and are interested enough to make a try."

Cayce's reference to the great work ahead of T.J., "provided of course that he has proper training in the formative years of his experience" was something no one in the family took lightly, and yet at times it must have felt like a Herculean effort that was impossible to achieve. Burlynn certainly had difficulty providing a stable environment for T.J. Not only did she have a craving for alcohol, but she was a single mother trying to hold on to a decent-paying job while raising a child on her own without the support of her husband or at times her other family members. She had become accustomed to working out her problems by escaping them—moving, breaking up with Boyd, getting back with Boyd, and repeating the process—unsure how to maintain her commitments, including to her own child.

Her addiction to alcohol had become more acute during her time in Montgomery, so much so that she wrote to Cayce on May 10, asking for another reading. "Physically I know what's wrong with me," she admitted. "I don't eat right and I have an awful appetite for beer that I wish I could check. I drink three or four bottles a day and I know it isn't good for me, but no matter how hard I try, I'll wind up 'so awfully hot and thirsty' that nothing satisfies me but beer. Isn't there some way besides will power to squelch such an appetite? It seems to me I've heard Gladys mention something, given in a reading."

But her drinking problem wasn't all that was on her mind. Reflecting on her previous life reading, which she acknowledged was requested out of "curiosity and blind faith," she was certain there was more to her life's purpose than what was revealed in that reading. "I feel that I've come over some pretty stormy territory since then but there's something in me that keeps telling me I've a job to do. What is it, I don't know."

Edgar made it clear to both Boyd and Burlynn exactly what their job was—to raise T.J. in the manner in which he could fulfill his destiny. Yet she wondered if she was supposed to be pursuing a career as a nurse. "With this war coming on," she wrote, "it's become more insistent. In one of my incarnations I was a nurse; do you suppose I'm to become one again? That was in the Egyptian period I believe when you were a priest."

She knew that if she became a wartime nurse, however, she would put herself in harm's way. She started to make arrangements for a caretaker for T.J. should something happen to her, even though she hadn't even begun to take nursing classes let alone volunteer for the armed services. Still, it is obvious she would only entrust her son to the Cayces. "Another thing, if anything should happen to me—such as my nursing in a war—would you take Thomas Jefferson," she asked in that same letter. "Of course this sounds a little futuristic but I've a feeling it won't be long until we're in it up to our necks. And with the possible future our baby has—he must not be raised by anyone who is not familiar with this information and who does not believe in it. By that I mean my family. I love them sincerely but I think you understand how I mean this."

What Burlynn could not have known at this juncture was the irony of her request. She may have insisted that the only one raising T.J. be someone who would enable him to attain the possible future Cayce's reading proposed, yet she and Boyd would be the ones whose decisions would ultimately prevent that from happening.

Edgar sensed something was awry and wanted to see for himself the situation surrounding T.J.'s family life. He and Gertrude went to visit the family in late May and had a chance to see Burlynn and T.J., but not Boyd.

Edgar and Gertrude visiting T.J. in Montgomery, Alabama, May 21, 1940.
(ECF#1166)

Their visit had a very strong impact on Burlynn. Writing to Mae Gimbert, Burlynn said: "The Cayces have gone and I feel awful. I don't remember when I've been as happy as I was while they were here. They stayed all nite with me in my little old two rooms when they could have stayed in any one of a dozen of the 'swankiest' homes in Montgomery that was open to them. I couldn't love those two people any more if they were my own family. . . Thomas Jefferson needs attention and I'm going to bring him up there for observation (readings and treatment) and I want to see whether I should stay up there or come back here with Boyd . . . Tell Gladys I'll bring her baby up as soon as I get the reading. Boyd says it's ok."

That same day, Burlynn wrote to Edgar and said Boyd was disappointed he missed seeing the Cayces, but she did not specify what kept him from home, other than to say, "He said if he had known you all were here all nite he'd have come on home." Burlynn promised Cayce she would bring T.J. up to Virginia Beach as soon as she got her reading. T.J., however, was under the impression he would be leaving with the Cayces, as that is what he had told his father. When the boy came into the room, he asked his mother if they were leaving, adding that he did not want to wait for school to be over.

Edgar echoed T.J.'s disappointment in a letter he wrote to Boyd on May 24 after their return to Virginia Beach. "Sorry to have missed you both in Selma and at your home. Would like to have seen and talked with you, for haven't heard from you since saw you here last summer. Hope Boyd you won't think me meddling when say the things am prompted to say here from having been at your home while you were away—was very much tempted to bring Thomas Jefferson home with me, but didn't think it was right to do so without talking with you about same. He looks pretty good, but isn't in good shape at all. Think he needs some attention bout the adenoids, and if you will let him come up here will do my best to have it looked after, if you think it a good thing to have done at this time. Feel sure between Miss Gladys and I we can have Dr. Richardson take care of it and get him in fine shape for this fall and winter. Don't know that this fits in with your and Burlynn's plans at all but am anxious about the boy as you know, each of us here think as much of him as if he belonged to us, and it is because am anxious about his health that am saying this, so if it is at all practical in any way for you all to let us try and get this all straightened out will be more than glad to do so."

The next day, Edgar wrote to Burlynn: ".… seems most a dream that we were actually there just a day or so ago. Was good to see you and that precious boy. What did he have to say when he came home? Wrote Boyd and hope he takes it as it was meant. Am hoping it will be practical for you to get up this way real soon."

With his and Burlynn's letters crossing in the mail, Edgar wrote her again on May 27. "What did Thomas Jefferson have to say when he got home and we were gone? . . . Wish might have seen Boyd, but possibly there is a reason. Will be looking for you and Thomas Jefferson, and do hope Burlynn you will come to me at any time and talk over with me any thing that comes up—you know am glad to try and help if possible and still think you a part of my job, but can't do much about it unless you let me know and let me try and help wherever and whenever can. Miss Gladys was disappointed of course that Thomas Jefferson didn't come but is anxiously awaiting your coming now. Thank you Burlynn—know am not much good but trying to help where ever and when ever I may—know of myself can do nothing, but in *Him* and through *Him* help may do much. All were glad to hear from you this morning—and think each of us filled up a bit, especially when T.J. said didn't want to wait till school was out. His lines say a whole mouthful."

Even before Cayce's letter arrived, Burlynn made arrangements to bring T.J. back to the Beach on June 1. While she was less than enthused about returning to Virginia, she knew he needed medical treatment and felt the move was the right thing to do.

Once again, T.J. was reunited with his beloved "Cakie" and once again, he enjoyed a summer in a stable home surrounded by members of his soul family who were devoted to him.

"This was typical of the tug-of-war that was a way of life for me during my childhood," T.J. said. "Most of the time I wasn't gone long enough for it to matter."

On June 5, 1940, Burlynn, along with T.J., Gladys, Gertrude, and Mrs. [1523] were present for a Check-Life reading that Cayce gave to Burlynn. Among other things, the reading made it clear what she and Boyd had to work out together in this life and what their obligations were to

T.J.

So, their individual opportunities, individual problems, should be lost in their desire, their purpose, to give, to be, in their relationships one with another, that which will give that entity who is a part of themselves the opportunity, the privilege, the possibility of fulfilling that destiny to which they have, in their associated capacity, committed themselves.

Thus that which is in keeping with those influences of a spiritual, a mental and material nature, should be directed - as should their activities - in giving that influence, that environment, that force and power, to that problem which is theirs in the present experience.

It is true that there may be delegated others, or relegated to others the opportunities to share in a portion of the activities to create the proper environment, in bringing into the experience of the entity the possibilities. However, the *responsibility* of same is *theirs* - the parents' (934-7, T9–11).

At the end of that reading, they asked whether

Cayce's Source had any other advice to give them at this time. The response was to the point: "Analyze thy purposes, thy hopes. Ye have been entrusted with a great opportunity. Do not fail thyselves, thy son, and - most of all - thy God" (934-7, T27).

Chapter Five

1941: "A Jumbled Up Affair"

Boyd Davis in uniform in England. (ECF#1256)

Faced with limited opportunities and growing debt, Boyd enlisted in the army in early 1941. Unbeknown to him, this would signal the beginning of years of separation between him and T.J. On February 11, Gladys made a notation in the file, explaining his reason for enlisting, writing that "he felt that at least his allotment check for his wife and son would be welcome, and he would have his living expenses and be doing something worthwhile."

Meanwhile, unaware that Boyd had enlisted, Burlynn wrote to him on February 7 with some rather harsh words, accusing him once more of shirking his responsibility as a husband and parent. Pleading for help to buy food and clothing for T.J., she seemed resigned to getting nothing from Boyd.

"You've never been much help financially and I stopped looking to you for it about two years ago, but there may come a time when you'll wish you had put a little more effort towards the responsibility of maintaining a home," she wrote.

Within days, Gladys told Burlynn that Boyd had enlisted and Burlynn's tone changed dramatically, going so far as to tell her husband she was proud of him. "To do what you have done takes courage because I'm sure you realize the seriousness of it," she wrote. "Take care of yourself Boyd. Perhaps after this miserable war is over we can find happiness. I'll try hard to take care of our boy and help him to fulfill his destiny."

Burlynn once again entertained the idea of returning to the Beach. "I can make more there and the environment is more constructive and influential for T.J.," she wrote. But Burlynn knew the pattern and admitted to Gladys, "It's hard for me to know what to do. I just ask in my prayers at nite to be guided and I'm doing my best to do what will lead to the greatest spiritual development for my boy. Gladys, this month I've grown closer to him and I know that I can give him the training he needs. I understand him better than anyone else does. He's easy to train and he's a good boy. I love him better than anything else in the world."

Two days later she wrote to Gladys again, assuring her that she would return to Virginia Beach provided she had a job. There was an opportunity for her to open a soda fountain, but she did not have the money to do so. She found this turn of events somewhat ironic, saying Boyd had the money and no place; she now had the place but no money. "It seems that destiny is tossing us around to suit herself," she wrote.

The magnitude of Boyd's enlistment had started to settle in, and Burlynn confided to Gladys that the news hit her like a thunderbolt and brought the seriousness of the nightmares of war to her doorstep. "The more I think of Boyd in the Army, the heavier my heart gets," she wrote. "It hurts to think that my husband and my son's father might be sent away somewhere to kill and destroy when that is the very thing our boy is destined to put to an end."

For her part, Gladys was sending Burlynn as much money as she could in support of T.J. Burlynn was staying with her mother, who could not afford to feed all three of them. Burlynn was willing to go back to her old job provided Boyd sent her the fare to return to Virginia. She not only needed that job, but she needed room and board for the two of them, as well as someone to look after T.J. while she worked.

As her desperation mounted, she sought solace from the one soul who encouraged her to come to him with whatever was troubling her—Edgar Cayce. In a letter dated February 27, 1941, she was candid in what her life had been like with Boyd, including the realization that she had the full responsibility of molding T.J.'s character.

That same day, Boyd wrote to Gladys: "My life has really been a jumbled up affair and naturally there are lots of things that I feel sorry about, especially my boy, but I'd rather not even think about it because it's a long, long way from the conditions I would like to exist. He'll be all right though because he will be able to take it, and hand it out too. I only wish we could have known each other at least."

Cayce answered Burlynn's letter immediately, telling her how glad he was to hear from her, reiterating again that he was "very sure you are one of my jobs, and will always do the best possible as I see it, tho may not always agree with others, hope can stay in your good graces. Would be awful to be in the doghouse with you."

Cayce reassured Burlynn that while Boyd did come to talk to him about her and T.J. several times before he joined the army, it was always amicable. " . . . never in all my life heard him say one unkind thing about you only he didn't understand you, yet, knew he loved you as he would never love another soul. Here this time any way. Have wondered at myself, and is possibly why I feel something of a guilty conscience, but after he iterated all the things about not hearing from you, not knowing what you were going to do and the like—I advised him that possibly a year in the Army would be the best thing for each of you. So possibly you have to blame me for his being in the Army,--then you very naturally would ask what I thought you were going to do, that I can't answer right of the reel, maybe can't until see and talk with you again, but assure you will help whatever way I can, while haven't any money—and that to the most of us seems to be the problem each day, for things have been and are terribly short here, but there are very properly much that is as important as money, at least you know my love and good wishes will be with you—and council if that is ever worth anything, so when you come back will wish to talk with you if I may and will see what can be done at all times. The lady from the school will be here the week end of the 14th or on the 14th and stay over Sunday, she has said she didn't think she could take T.J. just yet would have to wait until he was nearer ten or there about, will talk with her tho . . . hug and kiss T.J. for me and let me hear from you whenever you have the chance—and don't tear the others up. With love from all, EC."

The lady from the school that Cayce wrote about was Mrs. Beulah Emmet, founder of the New Mowing School, who would end up being one of the central players in T.J.'s life. (See chapter 9.)

Burlynn knew she had to do something—and fast—for herself and for T.J. She mentioned several times that T.J. and his grandmother did not get along well, and she also felt pressured by her mother to leave, but without the fare to get home, she was stuck. In her mind, she was constantly running numbers, trying to figure out the bare minimum they could live on. When she thought too much about it, she felt "like going raving mad."

But rather than go to the Beach, she and T.J. ended up in Cleveland where she got a temporary position at the board of education. The job gave her enough money to send T.J. to a day boarding school where he was given a warm lunch. Boyd sent her money but assumed it would be used to return to Virginia.

When T.J. became ill again, Burlynn tried to do what she could to provide remedies recommended in his previous health readings, but by spring, it was her own health that was in jeopardy. Boyd wrote to Gladys on April 5, expressing concern about Burlynn's eyes. "If she doesn't stop drinking beer she's liable to lose both eyes I'm afraid. I've seen them pretty bad before from that."

Burlynn continued to implore Boyd to send money, assuring him it wasn't for her, but for their son. She was fearful that something might happen to her while she was so far from the Cayces and Gladys and there would be no one to look after T.J. as she'd be flat broke. She wanted to save for the future, but could scarcely make ends meet. She worried that after the war there would be even fewer jobs and no security.

In an April 4 letter to Boyd, she wrote: "This may seem like I'm looking awfully far ahead but I feel like I've been warned by some intuition—anyway something I can't explain tells me to find my place in this affair and provide for the future of Thomas Jefferson. I've got to prepare him for the work that the readings say is his destiny. I know in my heart that he has a great work ahead of him and he is dependent upon you and me for the next few years for the necessary guidance and help for his development."

The situation with her eyes grew dire and by April 8, she was writing to Gladys and Edgar that she had a setback and was asking for a check reading.

"My eyes are all swollen especially my right one and it pains terribly. I can just barely see out of the left. I've got to get well soon. Ruby is just about dead and I'm pretty sure T.J. is getting the measles, although they haven't come out on him yet. I'm afraid I've lost my job but I might be able to get it back if I can get ok again. I'm so worried about my eyes . . ."

She was more worried than her letter implied. Writing to Boyd on the same day, she told him that she was unable to see out of one eye because it was swollen and red. T.J. was sick in bed and she was out of money, having spent it all on medicine and doctor appointments. "I'm scared Boyd," she admitted. "It's so awful to be sick away from Cayces. I don't know whether they'll keep my job for me or not. I hope so but I can't work before next week anyway. I can't see except out of my left eye. . . Please send us what you can, honey. We certainly need it. . . I'm so sorry to worry you darling but I need you so much."

Burlynn's fears were expressed further in a follow-up letter to Edgar on April 14, asking that if anything happened to her that he and Gladys would look after T.J. While her family loved him, they knew nothing of the future that Edgar planned for him. Her concerns about being away from the Cayces when she or T.J. was ill was partially due to the fact that her family did not believe in, nor follow, the Cayce remedies and chastised her for doing so.

"It's awful to be ill and away from you all and among people who scoff and ridicule what you know to be the only thing that can help," she had written earlier.

She had reason to be concerned that when her back was turned her family would take T.J. to a medical doctor and follow his prescription rather than a Cayce remedy. She fought against her family's insistence that she and T.J. be treated by a medical doctor and continued to apply the Cayce remedies, albeit sometimes in secret. She told Gladys that once when she was forced to see a medical doctor for the problems with her eyes, she ran into the ladies' room at the doctor's office to first apply the Cayce recommended mutton tallow compound he prescribed in her April 17 check reading (934-10) before she saw the doctor for one of his treatments.

For this and other reasons, Edgar urged Burlynn to

return to Virginia Beach. He and Gladys sent the reading to Burlynn, along with presents for T.J., one dollar, and a bottle of Atomidine, a product designed as an antiseptic for cuts, sores, infections, insect bites, and skin rashes. At times it was recommended in the readings to be taken internally in minute doses as a glandular stimulant and purifier.

Typing "blindly" on a typewriter she had borrowed from work to practice on, she acknowledged receipt of everything and expressed her gratitude. On the bright side, she shared the news that she had a job offer from Tony Jordan to work as a hostess at a Virginia Beach nightclub. Besides her regular salary, if she worked overtime, she'd bring in an additional $10 to $15. That kind of money was hard to turn down.

"Don't say anything about this to Boyd until I get there and am working," she cautioned Gladys. "If he knew I was making that much he might neglect sending the boy's money. And I will need it because it is so expensive there at the Beach."

But like most jobs Burlynn typically acquired at the Beach, she was given limited time before having to report to work and often missed those deadlines because of health reasons or because she could not afford the fare back to Virginia. For his part, Cayce urged her to reconsider the job Tony Jordan offered her, saying he was "afraid of the Nite Club. Be more money BUT would cost you more than 3 times as much to live in that atmosphere. And you would never see your child. Think of that. And as you said before he needs you else he would not have come to you."

Burlynn wrote back to Cayce, saying she agreed with him and would not take the job, but it wasn't up to her as she led Cayce to believe. In actuality, the job offer had been withdrawn since she did not return to Virginia on time. As if to make this loss easier to accept, she told Cayce she felt a restaurant job of any kind would put her in the same situation, but said she'd take a waitressing job until divine providence stepped in and led her to something better.

"I realize that I have a great responsibility to my son and I welcome it, but I'm also the breadwinner and I KNOW again that God will guide and help me," she wrote to Cayce on May 4. She said she would be at the Beach around mid-June, right after school was out and her job at the board of education ended. She was confident she could get that same job again when school started in the fall, indicating that she intended only to spend the summer at the Beach. She knew Virginia Beach was the root of all evil for her, telling Gladys she looked forward to returning to her job at the board of education in the fall because "it would be such a relief to be away from the sort of environment in which I have always been thrown there at the Beach."

By mid-May, Edgar felt he had been separated from T.J. so long that he worried the boy might forget about him. Writing to Burlynn, he said: "Guess T.J. will grow out of our knowledge, glad that he will be here this summer possibly get acquainted again." He added that "the lady who wishes to see him," that is, Beulah Emmet, would be there June 9 and would stay for several weeks. Edgar expressed the hope Mrs. Emmet would have some time to spend with T.J.

Burlynn may have sensed the need for a stronger male role model in T.J.'s life than Boyd because she admitted her nearly five-year-old son was becoming "a little headstrong and needs discipline badly. Ruby is so easy with him, he practically runs her. He also knows every kid on the street and they all congregate in our yard and it nearly drives her nuts." This ability to draw people to him would continue the rest of his life.

After not hearing from Boyd in a month, Burlynn was beginning to worry about her husband's activities. "I am a little afraid that he might have gone to town and had a little too much to drink and failed to show up at the proper time," she wrote on June 1.

Burlynn assured Gladys that when they arrived at the Beach, T.J. was "well prepared." Saying she had spent all but four dollars of her pay on clothes for him, she warned Gladys that he was very proud of his wardrobe and that no matter what, Gladys should not say anything about his clothes. "He likes them a little too well and struts a little too much," she said. "When he starts preening, just tell him he looks nice and let it go at that." Ironically, seventy years later, T.J. still identified himself as a "cool dresser."

While it may have seemed to Burlynn that Boyd

was not concerned about T.J.'s welfare, in fact he took out a life insurance policy with T.J. as beneficiary and arranged for a $20 monthly allotment to be sent to Gladys, rather than Burlynn, for reasons he explained in a June 13, 1941, letter to his sister: "Gladys, I am sending you a Life insurance policy that I took out and I'm going to try to raise it to $10,000, it's only a $1,000 now, but with a $10,000 policy he could get $50 a month the rest of his [life] in case something happened to me. I'm also sending an allotment of $20 a month to you for him. I know that won't take care of all his expenses but it'll help. I've been sending it to Burlynn but the last payday I had exactly $7.50 left after paying all my expenses and couldn't send her anything and she wrote me a pretty nasty letter about it and also one to my commanding officer . . . I'm afraid I made a big mistake several years ago in not taking T.J. away from her when I could have easily enough."

Gladys wrote back to Boyd on June 27, telling him that Burlynn and T.J. had arrived on the seventeenth and had a room in the home of Mrs. Bailey in Oceana that was "almost in front of Mrs. Gimbert's, next door to Mr. Butt (of Virginia Beach grocery) on one side, and the new Methodist minister on the next side who has three little boys young enough to play with Thom Jeff."

Gladys personally knew Mrs. Bailey and described her as "a nice lady." In addition to the room, Mrs. Bailey was caring for T.J.—all for $9.00 a week. There was a large backyard and T.J. played outside from morning until night. Gladys called it "an ideal location for him." Mrs.

Bailey had a daughter around fifteen and a son around twelve who were both "crazy about Thos. Jeff., and you know how easy it is for him to make himself one of the family."

It did not take Burlynn long to find employment, albeit out of desperation, as she took the kind of job Cayce warned her to avoid—as a hostess at the Lynx Club, which was a gambling house behind the Cavalier. She got $25 a week, but had to buy evening clothes and pay for board. She worked nights, but was expected on occasion to be there in the afternoon.

"Maybe she will get enough night life this way," Gladys wrote to Boyd. "When it's your bread and butter, I imagine it soon begins to lose its attraction."

While Gladys reported that Burlynn brought T.J. to her quite often, living in Oceana was a definite plus. "It will make her stay with him more," she told Boyd. "She is 'doing' his clothes, whereas if he were here I'd have it to do and she would be relieved of responsibility in all aspects, and probably wouldn't even see him once a week—she went that long last summer without seeing him. It is good for her to have the responsibility; besides, I think I can do more for him by being with him as much as I can when I'm not burdened with taking care of him physically and being worried to death all the time. However, you can be assured that if things don't go smoothly I can always 'take over.'"

At this point, it had been months since Boyd had last seen T.J. and Gladys encouraged her brother to come to the Beach to see him soon. "Six months is long enough to not see you," she wrote. She thanked Boyd for the insurance policy, "because we do want his education assured and that would do it."

Gladys had become Boyd's lifeline to his son, as he told his sister in a July 1 letter that his repeated calls to Burlynn were left unanswered. "I made three phone calls down there on his birthday but never did get in touch with Burlynn."

While he was glad she had a job, like Cayce, Boyd was concerned about the type of work she was doing. "I can't say that I think much of her choice," he wrote Gladys. "The place she works is nothing but a gambling den and her job is to get all the suckers to lose their money. However, she is good at that and she might not get caught. It would be pretty embarrassing for her if the law happened to raid the place some nite."

As for his son, Boyd admitted he wanted to see T.J. more but was afraid it would only make things worse than they already were. "The longer I stay up here (Ft. Meade) or in the Army rather, the more sure I am that there isn't much chance of ever getting out again. The Navy has been carrying on undeclared war for two months and I notice that a few of the senators in Washington are just finding it out. I learned about it from a sailor direct just what they've been doing and it wasn't playing soldier. I might break down and come down later on in the summer but I won't be able to stay very long. Give my regards to Mr. Cayce and hug T.J. for me."

Boyd began expressing doubt about whether his marriage would survive this separation. Writing to Gladys on August 5, he said he really didn't care about Burlynn anymore and would be satisfied with the end of their marriage as long as she took care of T.J. "I'm not blaming her for anything and there are not hard feelings toward her at all but enough is enough and I think I've had just that. Tell Thomas Jefferson that I think about him a lot and for him to be a good boy."

Burlynn returned to Ohio where she somehow secured a loan for the down payment on a small restaurant she wanted to open at the Beach. "It's going to be a first-class place and I believe that I can really establish myself and make some money, at least a nice living and feel that I can contribute to Thomas Jefferson's future," she wrote to Gladys. "I'm so thrilled over this new development. . . . It looks like I've finally got something that I can grasp with both hands and feel secure."

The last correspondence from Burlynn in 1941 was a letter she wrote on September 30 to Gladys. Her enthusiasm for her new restaurant venture was still high, telling Gladys she had a good down payment for her equipment and to acquire her license, anticipating the business would be in full swing by the following summer.

Meanwhile, Boyd was unaware of Burlynn's business plans and was surprised to learn that T.J. had been taken back to Ohio. This only increased his suspicions about her.

"She has been poison to me long enough and I do

hope that she does get a divorce," he wrote to Gladys. "I'm sure that it will be better for T.J. in the long run."

Gladys, like Edgar, treasured every moment she had with T.J. so having him at the Beach was an endless source of joy. Writing to her mother on October 29, Gladys shared insights into T.J.'s behavior that would have delighted any grandmother to read.

Boyd, on the other hand, felt cut off and powerless as far as T.J. was concerned. Since he was unable to see him in person, his only course of action was to write his son a letter in the hope that someone would read it to him.

In mid-October, Gladys asked Mr. Cayce to give another health reading for T.J. as he continued to battle colds and had difficulty breathing through his nose. When Cayce began the reading, his Source noted that he was not where he was supposed to be, and Gladys made a notation that the schoolmistress confirmed he was on the playground at the time of the reading. Cayce's ability to always know exactly where T.J. was would save the boy's life on several occasions.

By the first of November, Boyd was in Charlotte, North Carolina. Writing to T.J. he explained he could not write very often because most of the time he was "out in the woods sleeping on the ground on a lot of bushes" and teased his son that the boy probably would consider that fun for a while, especially the part about not bathing very often.

T.J. wrote back to his father as best he could, with Boyd acknowledging, "you are writing better and better each time I get a letter from you." Boyd told his son to "do everything Gladys and Cakie tells you to do and please don't ever tell them a story—always tell the truth to everyone. Bye and remember that daddy loves you more than anything in his life. Write to me soon."

Boyd's words earlier to Gladys that he had gotten Burlynn out of his system seemed to be true as he announced that he had fallen in love with Evangeline (Vangie) Garr, a young woman from an evangelical family who taught Sunday school every week. She did not drink, smoke, or dance, was a very good athlete "and about the healthiest person I've ever seen in my life." He said she was very attractive, played church and classical pieces on the piano, and even convinced him to attend church services.

"The thing that will be hard to believe is that she has kept me from drinking even a beer since I met her," he told Gladys. He said he told her all about T.J. and confessing his love for her, he was confident the feeling was mutual. "I know my heart is much lighter than it has been for years and it makes me feel so good in more ways than one," he wrote. "About an hour after I met her I knew something was different from what it usually is when you meet a person. I'm pretty sure that we knew each other in the Egyptian period."

For Boyd, Vangie was everything he could hope for in a woman and because of her, he was hopeful that his future would be bright. He was eager for his family to meet her but also anxious. Vangie planned to go to Norfolk to visit a friend and Boyd wanted to arrange a meeting, but expressed concern that it would be impractical or senseless for them to meet at this time. He was worried Burlynn would show up unexpectedly and ruin their meeting.

"It wouldn't matter except she might say or do something that would hurt someone's feelings for just the fun of it and I don't want that to happen at any time. I'm going to try and meet her in Norfolk when she comes, so maybe you could come in to meet her, though I'd like for her to meet Mr. Cayce and the rest, especially T.J."

But at that time, meeting the new woman in his father's life was not as much of a priority for T.J. as getting through an operation to remove both his tonsils and adenoids. Gladys noted, "The M.D. who performed the operation said the child had the worst case of adenoids he had ever seen and that it was a very difficult operation which verified the reading statement in 1208-16, Par. 9-A."

Boyd was not informed about the surgery ahead of time, so it came as a surprise when he learned about it after the fact. Nonetheless, he was glad it was done and that his son was all right. He said he would not be there for Christmas, but hoped to visit before the New Year.

Chapter Six

1942: "The Most Harm to Undo"

T.J. and his cousin Ann saluting, 1942. (ECF#1258)

Boyd did get to Virginia Beach the night of January 1, 1942. He had hoped to have a heart-to-heart with Edgar, but found the Cayces asleep. Two weeks later, he wrote to Edgar, saying: "I would like you to know I enjoyed my visit there very much and appreciate what you are doing for me in watching over TJ as you are. Some day I'm sure he will repay you and everyone that has had a hand in his correct development by living his life just as you expect him to, for other people rather than for himself, and you know he will be capable."

Reflecting on his father's letter, T.J. later said: "Again, everything was in place for me to fulfill Mr. Cayce's prophecy about the life I had ahead of me, but despite this level of assured anticipation, my 'correct development' never happened."

Cayce was still hopeful, writing back to Boyd on January 23: "You know we are all glad to do what we can toward looking after T.J. He is a fine fine little fellow. May we all give him the opportunity he deserves and am sure he will make his mark in the world."

But two days later, Boyd replied with a whole new set of problems. His relationship with Vangie had ended and he now was involved with a dancer who entertained the troops. She had a three-year-old son and was still married but her husband left her a year earlier. She and Boyd had become intimate and now she was pregnant. Since her symptoms were similar to Burlynn's health issues prior to her hysterectomy, Boyd asked Cayce to do a reading for her, but then added, "If you had rather not and think it's wrong please write and tell me so."

Cayce begged off, saying he already had so many readings to do that he did not think he could find the time to squeeze her in. He told Boyd he felt things would work out, but if they didn't, to let him know and he'd see what he could do to help. Nothing more was said about it.

Meanwhile, Boyd was not aware that Burlynn had started divorce proceedings. On January 28, 1942, Gladys made a notation that Burlynn had, in fact, obtained a decree for divorce, but subsequently Boyd's lawyer advised that she could not be granted the divorce without Boyd's consent, and that Boyd could claim custody of T.J.

Writing to Gladys on February 13, Boyd said the divorce " . . .was quite a shock since I haven't heard anything at all from anyone concerning it. I found out though that a divorce can be gotten that way if it isn't contested. There must not be any clauses relating to T.J. or I would have heard something I feel pretty sure. If she has gotten it and left him alone I'm really thankful and I expect she is satisfied with things as they are in that respect. . . Please do what you can in finding out if she is trying to take him for any length of time. It certainly wouldn't be very pleasant for him I don't think cause she'd never have time to look after him. . ."

As of March 9, Boyd still had not heard from Burlynn. It is unclear where she and T.J. were living at this time, but from his letter to Gladys, it sounded as though they were in nearby Oceana.

"I'm sorry that T.J. hasn't been able to stay out there and go to school, though," he wrote. "His environment probably isn't any too good out there where she is. Have you heard anything else about a divorce or do you think it was just a rumor she started or someone else started? The best thing to do I guess is just keep still and wait. There isn't anything else to do except start one myself and I still don't like the idea—let her do it. You can tell her that I'll give him a baseball glove and ball if he wants it. I'll mail it to you and you can give it to him. If I was you I don't think I'd start a fuss with her. It couldn't do any good and might do some harm. I'll also pay up Dr. Taylor—she needn't worry about that."

While Gladys was giving her brother regular updates, Boyd wrote to Edgar as well, knowing Cayce's concern for T.J. in the matter. Writing to Cayce on March 13, Boyd admitted he was very worried about what would happen to T.J. if Burlynn gained full custody.

"Personally, I think one of the main reasons she wants him is to help build herself up in other people's eyes. She is pretty good at drawing sympathy from folks. I would like to know just what grounds she did use. The only deserting that has ever been done was by her, not me, and about a dozen times at that. However, that's neither here nor there. What I want is that child and if I have to do it the hard way I think I can but I'd rather not if it can be avoided."

Boyd confessed to Gladys that wondering what was happening back in Virginia Beach had him "all mixed up." He couldn't find a way to get T.J. back unless he went to court and he did not want to do that unless it was absolutely necessary. Yet he also felt that Burlynn really did not want T.J. and was holding on to him out of spite. "I can't believe yet that she cares enough for that kid to really want the responsibility of taking care of him—it just isn't in her," he wrote.

Boyd seemed more determined than ever to limit Burlynn's access to their son, even though he didn't have a clue how to do that. He told Gladys he did not mind if

Burlynn had T.J. for short periods of time, as long as she did not take him out of the state, and that he would agree for her to see him whenever she liked, but he definitely did not want her to raise him, "because I don't think she is capable at all." He hoped they could settle out of court, but added that his side would have to be "mighty smart and careful" because, "If she thinks they are trying to force her into giving him up she'll fight much harder to keep him."

Edgar gave Boyd a reading the following day, with Gertrude and Gladys in attendance. When asked how the divorce could be granted with the least harm to those concerned, Cayce's Source answered: "What's already been done is the most harm to undo, or to change. We may expect a great deal of animosity and hate, a great deal of things that may even lead to things that would be very questionable to many. Under the circumstances these may be expected" (391-19, T4).

A week later, Boyd wrote to Gladys and again expressed his hope that everything could be settled out of court. He was especially apprehensive about Burlynn getting wind of the fact that he was challenging her for custody of T.J. and he asked Gladys to keep that to herself.

He hoped he could come down the following week, but was doubtful Burlynn would allow him to see T.J. Nonetheless, he had some baseball-related and other gifts that he wanted T.J. to have so somehow he would find a way of delivering them.

He ended the letter by telling Gladys that he had

done some research about his rights as a member of the armed forces that would impact the proceedings. "The Sailors and Soldiers Act passed in 1940 will void that divorce altogether for the duration of the time I'm in the service, so it doesn't mean anything in the first place legally," he wrote on March 25. "If I have someone to represent me, however, and lose out then it's perfectly legal. I can't believe that Kellam [a local Virginia Beach lawyer] would take a case like that knowing the law as it is unless maybe they want me to contest it so that he will have a chance to win it. As things stand now she is still my wife. I don't think the Rdg had the divorce in mind when it said the worst has been done."

A month later, Gladys reported that things had improved with Burlynn and that she had paid for T.J.'s schooling the last two weeks and also offered to help pay for his board if Gladys wasn't getting anything from Boyd. Gladys opted to continue to maintain that secret, telling Boyd: "It really takes more than that to take care of him, and anything she gives can be used to advantage. I need to get a bed for him right now, as the cot is not comfortable."

Knowing Boyd was eager for anything Gladys could share with him about how T.J. was getting along, she gave him some detail about T.J.'s latest passion. "Wish you could hear Thos. Jeff. playing and talking to himself sometimes. He got a Donald Duck, or at least a Duck doll from Ruby at Easter, and he sleeps with it and plays with it. *So* I hear conversations that go something like this: 'Don't you know how to swim, son? It's like this.' And then he proceeds to show him. He plays like he's the daddy, you see, and his voice sounds exactly like yours.

"The Bailey's at Oceana have a lot of little chickens, so he has been tremendously interested—since Easter—in eggs and chickens, and how the little biddies hatch. I took him to Norfolk one day and we passed by a pet shop (accidentally, I assure you), and I thought I'd never get him away. He wanted to buy one of the baby roosters, especially. He kept asking me questions about how the eggs hatched. So the other day, he said, 'Gladys, if I sat on an egg a whole year, could I hatch a little biddie?' He can't understand why *he* can't do it, instead of having to depend on the hen. However, he can't sit still two minutes. That's why, I guess, that he thought maybe a whole year would do the trick."

Gladys ended the letter by saying their attorney, Paul Ackiss, indicated she needed the policy that named her as T.J.'s guardian so she could administer the money Boyd was sending for his son's needs and Burlynn would be unable to get at it.

On May 13, Boyd wrote to Gladys from Belvoir Hospital near Washington, DC, where he being treated for a back injury he incurred while wrestling at military camp. He assured Gladys the injury had nothing to do with his drinking.

Gladys wrote back on May 28, relieved that his condition was improving. Believing it would help with his healing process, Gladys was inspired to share more about what T.J. was up to while she cared for him. "Thos. Jeff. won *all* the prizes on his rabbit at the Pet Show last Saturday. There were about twelve prizes for rodents, and his was the *only* one there; consequently he got them all. Probably a hundred dogs were entered, but only his rabbit. I guess such a thing will never happen again, so I'm going to keep his ribbons in a scrapbook. He also won two prizes with his turtle; one as the smallest pet, and the other as the most unusual combination, as Eddie Cayce and I conceived the idea of representing The Hare and the Tortoise. He certainly did enjoy the whole procedure.

"His school will be out next Wednesday, so guess I'll be going to his commencement exercises (or what do you call them?). Did I tell you that he sang Deep in the Heart of Texas straight through with Cliff Edwards in the movies one day? He had all the audience in roars.

"The other night while saying his prayers he ended up with this: 'And God, please send my Daddy. For Jesus' sake, Amen.' What he meant by that I don't know, unless he meant for you to come and see him. He certainly can ask questions, and is beginning to—on all subjects—especially life and death, as he goes to bed at night. That's why I'm so glad to have him nights, so I can give him a spiritual slant on life in general. He accepts without question the fact that when he dies he comes back again as a baby. It is certainly the easiest way to explain death to children—by using nature as the example, how a plant dies and then comes up again next season. I got him to eat his grapefruit this morning by telling him that he breathes it out and the spirit of it goes into another young grapefruit."

In that same letter, she said their brother Burt had purchased a home and that they were all going to move into it as soon as the renters left.

Upon receipt of the letter, Boyd wrote to T.J. on May 30 from Fredericksburg, Virginia, to congratulate him on winning the prize ribbons at the animal show and telling him how much he wished he could be there to see him graduate from school.

Gladys decided to keep T.J. occupied through the summer by enrolling him in a play school on the beach every morning. There, she said, he would have the sun and the sand and could play games with other children. She explained that the program, under the Recreational Department of Virginia Beach, was supervised by trained personnel, but added that it was expensive—$1 per week and 50-cents bus fare, not to mention all the incidentals. "You know how your son can wiggle money out of you!" she told Boyd.

T.J.'s time on the beach had given him quite a tan and Gladys assured Boyd that his son was healthy and gaining weight, and that he had made friends with the Smithson boys who lived down the street. She added that he was eager for Boyd to come for a visit. Knowing Boyd's apprehension about showing up at the Beach, Gladys suggested he meet them at their sister Lucille's home in Norfolk.

The impact of the war was being felt at home and even a six-year-old child picked up on the who's who of the conflict. Typical of the witty things T.J. said, Gladys shared one, in particular, with Boyd that she found especially amusing.

"The other day he said, 'Gladys, we don't say Hi Hitler, we say Hi Uncle Sam,'" she shared in a letter dated June 10. "You know why? Because Hitler's our antackonist."

But that wasn't all he had to say. Telling Boyd that since Easter, T.J. had become interested in the hatching of eggs, the youngster had somehow connected the hatching of eggs with marriage and having babies.

"One day at the table, he said, 'Gladys, are you ever going to get married?' I said, 'I don't think so. Why? Would you like for me to get married?' 'Yes.' Mr. Cayce said, 'Who would she marry?' I said, 'Yes, who would I marry?' He thought a minute and then said, 'Eddie Cayce.' 'But Eddie Cayce is already married.' 'Well Gladys, if Eddie Cayce is married, why don't he hatch some eggs?'"

A week before T.J.'s sixth birthday, Gladys sent Boyd photos of his son, including one with him fishing with Mr. Cayce. "Tell Mr. Cayce to please not let him fall in the lake—that was one of the first things I thought about when I first looked at it, he was so close to the edge," Boyd wrote in his return letter, echoing something that T.J. would comment on later as an adult.

Boyd expressed the hope that he could see T.J. the following week for his birthday and accepted Gladys's invitation to stay with Lucille. There is no record of whether he made it back to see T.J., but by July 11 he was writing to Gladys from North Carolina, advising her that he may be moved yet again at any time. He explained how difficult it was for him to stay in touch, as he was part of the team that was feeding over four hundred troops, twenty-four hours a day.

By August he was in Florida at Camp Blanding. That same month, Gladys and T.J. moved in with her brother Burt, along with her mother, younger sister, her husband and four-year-old daughter.

Boyd had no inkling that the war was impacting T.J. until Gladys told him about the way she arranged the house so she could hear T.J. if he called out. "I've fixed the two upstairs rooms for Burt and me, mine being a single room and Burt's a double with twin beds," she wrote. "So Thos. Jeff. is now established in a man's room, with his little desk in one corner and his clothes in a drawer next to Burt's. It is right across a tiny hall from me, and I can hear him through the night if he calls. He was quite concerned the night of the last blackout, when some man on the street (just for fun, I guess, but we thought it was a policeman at first) yelled up at us to put the lights out—before the siren blew."

On September 22, Boyd wrote to Gladys that he was in a secret location and could not tell her where that was, but added that he could get mail if it was sent in care of the postmaster in New York City. He still had not been able to get away to see T.J. and it seemed doubtful that he would any time soon.

Back at home, the family was keeping abreast of the war efforts via the local movie theater. Gladys wrote to Boyd on October 17, 1942, telling him of T.J.'s reaction to what he saw. "Thos. Jeff. and I went to the movie late yesterday and there was the best newsreel of the war that I have seen thus far. It started with Hitler's first conquests and brought everything up to date. Thos. Jeff. said in the middle of all the fighting, 'It sure is a good picture, Gladys.' Last night in his prayers he said, 'God, please take care of Daddy, and help me to be a good boy so he'll be proud of me. Help Bubber to be good, and help everybody to be good. For Jesus' sake, Amen.'"

On November 9, Gladys wrote to Boyd, acknowledging receipt of his allotment check, which included an increase. She told her brother she intended to put some of it in a savings account for T.J. under her name so that Burlynn would not be tempted to "borrow" those funds for her restaurant business.

The following day she wrote to say that they had new neighbors who had moved in behind them. They had children—a boy about a year older than T.J. and a girl who was younger. They were "having a time" of it.

"Thos. Jeff. informed me this afternoon that he just had to go play with Terry; that they were building a fort. He really enjoys going to school. Last night I read to him quite a bit, and he put a book in his book bag to take to school with him, because 'Miss Bennett reads better than *anybody*!' He comes in and does his 'home work.'

Now he has Ann doing it. Lucille has taught her now to write her name, and she studies her lessons right along with him. They are awfully cute together. He asked Ann the other day if he couldn't be Big Brother to her Baby Brother when he came. They are quite mixed up about his coming, - as to whether God is sending him, Santa Claus is bringing him, or the Stork is dropping him, or whether he is to be had at the hospital. No wonder!"

In that same letter, Gladys told Boyd that Burlynn had a falling out with Mae and was now staying at the Moore Cottage. Gladys rarely saw Burlynn, however she talked to her once or twice a week on the phone as T.J. spent a few hours one afternoon a week and all of Sunday afternoon with his mother. Gladys took T.J. to the movies one afternoon a week, and read to him two or three nights. He and his cousin Ann had a "grand time" playing together after supper. "Sometimes it seems like that house is just a background for the children, and I'm glad—that is what I wanted it to be," she wrote.

On November 19, Gladys wrote to Boyd, telling him that T.J. was becoming quite popular. "He went to another birthday party yesterday afternoon. I'll bet no little boy gets invited to as many parties as he does."

She added that his reading skills were improving. "The other day he came running to me with a grown up book and said, 'Gladys, look here! Read me this story about *Dick*.' I looked and the word was *did*. He can hardly wait to be able to read the newspaper and such….."

With Christmas just a few weeks away, Gladys

assured Boyd that T.J. would have a wonderful holiday. "I think we will have a very nice time, with a Xmas tree all our own this year, and the two children together making it seem more like Xmas. …"

Throughout this, the family had not heard from Boyd. When he finally corresponded on November 24, it was a little surprising to find it was to Burlynn, and not Gladys. In the letter, he addressed the divorce: "I don't want you to think that I ever wanted to stop you from getting a divorce for any great reason other than to feel that T.J. was where I would feel free to come and be with him when and if I got out of this uniform. With you married to someone else and keeping him I'd hate to come around. You can understand that I hope. The main idea is to see that he's taken care of, tho - - -and not whether I can come and see him. Bless his heart, he's a swell boy. The last time I saw him he was just as mannish as could be and tried to act so grown up. He has an uncanny understanding, too. . . This is the first letter I've written in months so please tell Gladys and the rest I'm fine and not to worry. Please hug Thomas Jefferson for me and don't let him forget me completely."

Five days later he wrote to Gladys, prefacing that because he was restricted from what he could put in a letter, it was almost a hopeless job trying to make his letters very interesting. He said he would try to have a picture taken of himself so T.J. wouldn't forget what he looked like.

By December, Boyd was in England and Gladys

wrote to him shortly after Christmas, saying she was happy that is where he was sent, "for I'm sure it is better there than most any of the other war countries you could be in." She told Boyd the family had "about the nicest, homiest Xmas we've had in years" and added that Burlynn came and was getting on all right with the exception of having to wear glasses most of the time because she could not see out of both eyes. ". . . she continues to drink off and on—I hear it from various sources," Gladys wrote. "She was wearing a beautiful leopard fur coat. Thos. Jeff. goes out there to spend an afternoon or a day occasionally, - usually spends Sundays with her at the restaurant; otherwise he is with me all the time. He is growing like everything and so smart. It is a job to curb the little Alexander in him, however, as he is as bossy as can be with Ann, although he loves to play with her. But he always wants to win, no matter what game he plays. I want to try to get that necessity out of him if I can. Even Thos. Jeff. the Pres. had that trait, - never could stand to be defeated, or have anyone else outdo him.

"Shea makes a cross when he says the blessing at table, and last night when Thos. Jeff. said his prayers I noticed that he made the same kind of cross on his chest with his fingers—maybe he's been doing it all the time, but I only noticed it last night. He did it so naturally. He picks up everything under the sun that he sees anybody else do, and can copy it to a 't'. He makes the swastika on everything he owns—has even done it all over his desk. I looked the swastika up in a book on symbology that I have here, and it seems that it was used extensively in Greece during the period when he was Alexander. No wonder he can draw it so perfectly.

"I bought him a big blackboard from *you*, that hangs on the wall just like in a schoolroom, and Burt gave him the crayons and eraser to go with it—big box of chalk, etc. He had a *very* nice Xmas. Burlynn gave him an air raid warden raincoat and helmet. I'll take a picture of him in it and send to you.

"He received several books, and one I gave him that he can read himself—he is learning so fast. He's always spelling out words on boxes and things. Mrs. Cayce gave him a book with stories about the wonders of our country. I've read one story in it already that he liked very much; it was about the giant sequoia tree in California. It is written so entertainingly that the tree seemed like a human giant.

"......I'll take good care of your boy, and try to train him as best I can towards the things we believe in most. He wanted to know the other day, 'How did Daddy get that blackboard over here from England?' I told him you ordered it through Santa Claus, who had access to everything there is."

Chapter Seven

1943: "So Long Since I've Seen You"

Boyd and T.J. in front of the Star of the Sea and the Cayce yard, fall 1940.
(ECF#1153)

With the war raging in Europe, Gladys's concern for her brother's safety had infiltrated her dreams. Writing to Boyd on January 15, she described a dream she had about him that morning, adding that several hours later thousands of soldiers had marched by their home just as T.J. was heading off to school. He was wearing the air raid warden coat and hat that Burlynn had given him and Gladys said the soldiers talked to him as they passed by. T.J. came in and asked his aunt when his father would be coming home, writing "1943" on his blackboard.

In early February, T.J. came down with an earache, fever, and swollen glands, diagnosed as mumps. Gladys requested an emergency reading from Cayce, and the remedy worked so well that Gladys said she never saw "a case of mumps so easily and quickly cured." This would be the final reading Cayce would give for T.J.

T.J. had no sooner gotten over the mumps when he came down with the chicken pox. He had gone to spend the weekend with his mother in her new apartment in Oceana and he broke out the next morning. Burlynn kept him out of school until he got over the chicken pox, so it was two weeks before he returned to class. Nonetheless Gladys reported he went outdoors, to the movies, and everywhere in a few days as if he was never sick. He ended up with one mark on his face, in the middle of his nose between his eyes. Gladys said it was "rather distinguishing, like a dimple."

After nursing her son during his bout with chicken pox, Burlynn decided she liked having him there. Writing to Boyd on March 21, Gladys described the situation.

"During the time he was out there, Burlynn found that she liked having him and that the school hours in Oceana are between 10 and 4, which took care of him most of the day; so she proceeded to call me up and say she had decided to send him out there to school. Well, there was nothing I could do, and it may be just as well, as Lucy Hatchett is his teacher and apparently a very good one and he likes it fine, and she seems to have a special interest in him—but so did Madeline. Of course, I can see how Burlynn feels. He is her only real excuse for getting that apartment and fixing it up; I mean without him there wouldn't be any excuse—while if she has him with her she can say that she is making a home for him. Well, I wish you could see it. It is the upstairs Owen apartment, right next to Mrs. Baillo's, down the street a little from the Bailey's on the opposite side of the street—in fact, right in front and to the left of Mrs. Gimbert's. It is a four room apartment, very modern, and I'm sure she has spent at least a thousand dollars furnishing it—the very best of everything—luxurious is the word; like a N.Y. swell apt. She has asked me if I would come live with her, which of course I couldn't do—at least, I mean I wouldn't drop everything and depend on that—but I promised I'd come out there and stay with him nights during the summer, so she can keep the restaurant open late. I spend about one night a week with her already, and he comes to me a night or two through the weekend. She called me up the other night—Friday—and asked if he could come spend the night with me, that "Rabbit" (the first time she has ever mentioned him to me like that) had asked her to go in town for some chow mein. Apparently he comes to the apartment every evening. At least Mae says that he sees her every single night (or did while she was staying at Mae's, though not at the house, of course). One night I was out there and altho she had been after me to come spend the night, she apparently didn't want me to stay that night and phoned for a taxi for me; so I concluded it was because she had made arrangements for him to come see her after I left, and of course she couldn't call him while I was there to make new plans. So, Honey, that's the way it is. Of course, as you saw when you were here, she probably isn't happy—because the situation isn't exactly pleasant, and probably harder for her than most people, knowing he is married and there's nothing she can do about it. I believe that's one thing that keeps the affair alive, the very fact that she hasn't been able to completely control him as yet. I don't know why she doesn't write you exactly how she feels. But you know how she is, always wanting to have her cake and eat it, too. I'm sure she'd like to have you come back still wanting her, so she could hold it over his head.

"As you say, she is thinking only of herself and apparently not concerned about the fairness to you, leaving things 'up in the air' and not being definite enough to let you feel free to do as you like. Once right after your last letter to her came, I was talking over the phone to Thos. Jeff. and she was helping him write a letter to you. I hope it got mailed, and I hope she wrote one too."

With T.J. now living with his mother, Gladys was in a quandary about what to do with the allotment check that Boyd was sending her, which by now had grown to $50 a month. Remarking on how extravagant Burlynn had become, Gladys told Boyd his wife decided to buy a car. Gladys was concerned she would splurge on that as well.

"Cille and the Cayces all tell me it would be silly to give her any of the allotment money when she's spending like she is—it would just *go* and be nothing to show for it *for him* later," she wrote. "They advise me to put the money in a savings account for him. So please let me know what you wish me to do . . . Mr. Cayce still feels it would be the best thing for Thos. Jeff. if we could get him in Mrs. Emmet's school this fall, and there is a chance that Burlynn will consent—if the war is coming to an end by then, and I sincerely believe it will be. I know the environment out there with her isn't the best in the world, but it's not so bad while he's in school so much of the time; and I'll spend as much time with him as I can. We go to the movies about twice a week, and Ann is a part of our plans most of the time. He is crazy about her, and they argue back and forth *all* the time—*but like it*!

"Thursday night Thos. Jeff. stayed with me and had just pulled out a loose tooth, which he put under his pillow so the fairy would leave him a nickel for it. He has gotten a nickel so far for every tooth he's lost. Well, I almost forgot to get it and put the nickel—woke up in the night and remembered to attend to it. So under separate cover I am sending you his little tooth. I thought it would give you a thrill to see and touch something that had been such a part of him.

"That reminds me, I'm also sending you a copy of the regular edition of *There Is a River, The Story of Edgar Cayce* by Thomas Sugrue, as I know you'll want a copy. Thos. Jeff. has a copy of the limited edition, autographed with a special message, but I'm sending you one of the regular editions that has just come on the market…

"We are getting on fine here, - shoes have been rationed and all canned foods, cars, gasoline, fuel, etc; but all in all we haven't suffered yet in any real sense. I do hope you are getting on alright and not letting anything get you 'down.' You can be such an optimistic influence for others when you keep looking up yourself. Remember, you have a little boy who is thinking about you and betting on you. We talk about 'Daddy' every time we get together. Every now and then I hear him laying the law down to Ann, and he'll say, 'Yes it is, Ann, 'cause my Daddy said' so and so. Yes, he has a lot bigger appetite than he used to; he plays outdoors a lot and seems to have a real desire for food— asks for it, instead of us having to force it on him—seems to really like milk, too."

Boyd wrote back to Gladys and said he'd rather she continued to keep the money rather than give it to

Burlynn. He was going to raise the allotment to $100, with the stipulation that Gladys save some of the money for him so he'd have something when he got home.

On April 21, Gladys wrote to Boyd that T.J. was spending each weekend with her, being driven back and forth by Burlynn in her new car. Burlynn was busy remodeling her restaurant, putting in cafeteria-style service since it was too hard to get help. Even harder was affording food, as everything was being rationed except fresh vegetables and those were very expensive. Gladys said she had started a garden, and mentioned Mr. Cayce's garden was already going strong so she was sure they would not starve.

Having Boyd so far away was difficult for the entire family. Gladys implored him to write and tell her about what life was like in England. Meanwhile, she told him that T.J. was going around showing his muscles and boasting about how strong he was becoming. She occasionally heard him tell others that his daddy was in the army. She promised to sit him down that weekend to write his father a letter.

T.J. spent his Easter vacation with Gladys and kept her on the go. She took T.J. and Ann to the movies three days in a row. She told Boyd that she thought it was a good idea for her to save part of his allotment check for him because she believed things would not be easy when the war ended.

"I asked Thos. Jeff. how he'd like to run a farm with Daddy when he came back from the war," she wrote on April 26. "He was delighted at the idea. I read about the life of Thomas Jefferson, how he loved farming, and said, 'The people who work with the soil are God's chosen people, if He has a chosen people.' Already food is pretty scarce, at least it is TERRIBLY expensive—and some things we have taken so for granted are now extremely hard to get. However, Mr. C has a nice garden coming along and will do lots of canning, also Cille and Shay are starting a little garden in our back yard, as well as a little chicken yard. Thos. Jeff. & Ann go out and re-enact all the movies. They really do have fun playing together. He is getting taller and taller, but still doesn't broaden out much."

Gladys continued to give Boyd updates on T.J. On May 8, she wrote: "Your little boy is with me today, and we're leaving in a little bit to pick up Ann and go to our usual Western movie on Saturdays. It is quite a habit now, and Ann likes the Westerns best too. Thos. Jeff. has had a string of children here today playing, from all around the neighborhood, and we've had a time trying to keep them out of Mr. C's strawberry patch—which is just beginning to turn. You can just see the hospitality sticking out all over Thos. Jeff., he thinks everything here belongs to him anyway, you know, and this nice garden just fascinates him. He called my attention this morning to the fact that *his* pansies were blooming profusely. You remember, about two years ago he got a little pansy plant for Easter, and Mr. C. planted it out back here. It certainly has thrived. Also he takes such an interest in our garden at home now, that Cille & Shay have developed mostly, since I haven't had much time for it. We have onions, peas, beets, beans, butterbeans, saps, etc, coming along nicely. Also our fig trees are showing evidence of aliveness, a damson plum tree, and a couple of grape vines. Maybe I shouldn't be mentioning these, if it makes you hungry for something you can't get—but we can't get them either yet, but hope we will along about July and August."

The endless waiting for some word about the divorce reached its peak in June. Writing to Gladys a few days before T.J.'s seventh birthday, Boyd said he had met a "very sweet" woman that he was sure Gladys and everyone back home would approve of.

"She's real nice, doesn't drink or smoke, etc., and can have a very good chance of reforming me I think," he wrote. "Anyway, whether anything ever comes of it or not I want the divorce finished. I'm sure I'll never go back with her and I know that I do want to get married again and it'll probably be someone that's in a uniform or has worn one. There's a lot we have in common. Please do that soon as you can and... then I can see the Red Cross. They probably could handle the whole thing but it might not be so nice for her that way. You see, the girl won't even see me anymore until something is done about it and she's perfectly right."

On July 25, 1943, Boyd wrote to Gladys saying he received her letter concerning what attorney Paul Ackiss had to say about the divorce and that he already wrote back to him.

"I guess the only thing he can do is enter a counter suit altho' I never did want to do that unless I had to. Maybe everything will come out all right in the end, but I can't understand why she wants to try to take him from me that way. She hasn't shown any too much interest otherwise and I'm pretty sure she won't take care of him properly unless there has been some big change in her outlook on things in general. So much for that—all I can do is sit and wait now and hope for the best."

While Boyd awaited news on the divorce, T.J. was happily spending the summer with Gladys. He liked being at her home because he had a wonderful yard to play in that served as a magnet for neighborhood children. Gladys told her brother that T.J. enjoyed working around the yard, doing odd jobs, tending to the chickens and the garden. "He takes such an interest in everything we do to improve things," she said. Gladys added that her mother overheard T.J. telling the neighborhood children that Burlynn told him he'd be living with his father when he came back.

On that subject, Gladys told Boyd that Paul Ackiss said that unless Boyd wanted to fight it out in the courts regarding custody of T.J., he might as well consider himself divorced. "As the record now stands she has the divorce, and custody of him, altho she states in the record that you send money for his support," she wrote. "Mr.

Ackiss says that probably the less fuss made about it the better, and that we'll probably be able to do more for him by leaving things as they are. You know how she is; if she thinks we're fighting her or trying to take something away from her, then she will fight tooth and toenail; whereas, if we agree to everything we have a good chance to have him thrown on our hands continually, except occasionally when she wants to see him—when she is down and out, feeling lonesome or the like. Of course, she would never take care of him herself anyway, but delegate it to somebody else. So I don't really see that you have anything to gain by raising a fuss now—it should have been done long ago if at all. The way he is developing, he'll do as he pleases in a few more years—he almost does now. All we can do is try to give him as much home background and spiritual basis as possible. He is already big enough to realize that most of the time his mother is too busy or too preoccupied to want him around; in fact, he says so.

"Cille and Shay are friendly with her and visit with her a little bit now and then, which has changed her whole attitude about all of us at home—so that she drops in for a minute now and then, and sends down ice cream, etc, occasionally, and lets Thos. Jeff. stay there almost *all* the time. I've made it a point to agree with everything she ever says, it is always easier that way and quiets her right down if she is upset about something—just like a person demented, really. I do know it will all work out alright. She is getting real fat and sort of sloppy looking, and her face has a sort of coarse look—at least several people have expressed it that way, but I try not to think about her in that sense—only as Thos. Jeff.'s mother. So you do as you feel best, Honey, about the divorce business . . . I really believe the best thing to do now is to accept the divorce decree that she has been granted, and not fight it . . . You can still do all you can for Thos. Jeff., and perhaps even more than you could do if you antagonized her. As it now is, no question would be raised by her, since *she* is the one who has gotten the divorce, made the complaints in court, etc., and you just agreed to it by your silence. Let me know what you think." Boyd agreed.

Shortly thereafter, Gladys wrote to Boyd that Burlynn had decided to let T.J. stay with Gladys nights and go to the Beach school, as Burlynn would be working every night and it would suit her better to have T.J. in the afternoons. She said he was going to a movie nearly every day now and she expressed concern that it would hurt him to see so many of them.

"Mrs. Cayce said Hugh Lynn used to see every Wild West movie that came to town—used to go nearly every afternoon, and I don't suppose it has hurt him—altho H.L. himself told me he didn't think it was good for children to see all these war pictures," she wrote to Boyd. "I don't suppose it is, but he just loves them—and considering who he is, I guess most all of it is 'old stuff' to him anyway, just presented in a little more modern version. One of our members sent us some books on Thos. Jeff. – his personal notes, etc. – four volumes, printed in

1829. You'll enjoy reading them when you come back."

By the end of September, Boyd wrote to Gladys that the English girl he had been so infatuated with had been transferred and he hadn't heard from her since. He said he didn't pursue other women because either he didn't seem to care for their company or else he was just difficult to please.

With Christmas a few months away, Gladys told Boyd that T.J.'s idea of perfect Christmas presents for his father were all army related. Boyd wrote back asking Gladys to tell T.J. to not insist on anything military for him—he had had enough as it was. He said he thought western movies were fine and would be good for him, but cautioned Gladys to keep an eye on him when he was on the streets. "I think about those Army trucks a lot because I know how most of the fellows drive them—make him be very careful."

Gladys encouraged Boyd to write to T.J. as the boy had said he wasn't going to write to his father unless his father wrote back. Boyd promised to do so and wrote to T.J. on September 24.

"My Dearest Son,

"Since this is my first letter to you I'm wondering just what to talk about. I know someone will have to read this to you so there can't be any secrets in it. We'll have to wait until you learn to read and write yourself for that.

"I suppose you have in mind a lot of things you would like to have for Christmas so let Gladys know and she will let me know and we'll see if you can't get them. You must be a pretty big boy by now. It's been so long since I've seen you that I can't very well imagine your size except compare you with some of the boys over here your age and I know quite a few of them. One is a little boy by the name of Jimmy and I see him pretty often. He has a lot of little baby rabbits and we play with them every time I go to see him. He is a good little boy too and very polite as little boys should be. Here in camp we have three solid black cats and one of them is going to have some little baby kittens soon. They should be all black too but you never can tell. They'll probably be part spotted or something.

"I have some pictures I'm sending but they're not very good. If we can ever get any films I'll try to take some decent ones to send to you.

"Well, son, I'm closing now and there's no need to tell you that I miss you more than anything in the world and am looking forward to seeing you again, so be a good boy as always and study hard in school so you will be smart when you grow up. Do everything that they tell you to do and don't complain about anything. Keep yourself happy and always be nice to other people at all times.

"Please write to me and tell me all about what you are doing and what's happening back there.

"Bye for now with all my love, Daddy."

Chapter Eight

1944: "The Little Every Day
Living That Gets You"

Burlynn and T.J. in front of Bama Boys, her refreshment stand at 14th and Atlantic.
(ECF#1152)

The last full year that the Davis and Cayce families were together was 1944, for early in 1945 Edgar Cayce's death would forever change their lives.

Boyd was still stationed overseas and did what he could to support his family. At this point, he had not seen T.J. in nearly three years and he had no idea when they would be reunited. He told Gladys he wasn't sure where he would live when he returned to the states, but he didn't think he'd settle in Virginia Beach.

"Just think," he wrote about his son. "Eight years old. It doesn't seem possible that it could be that long. He'll be a half grown man when I see him again. It certainly will make me feel old, I know. This is the time when I should be with him too and not years later. With all my faults there are still a lot of things I could help him with, even tho' I know he has the best of care in every way."

By late June, Boyd's greatest concern was the war. His unit was on the front lines now and in a letter to Gladys, he described what it was like to be in that combat zone. "There's one thing about it, we don't get lonesome at nite because of silence," he wrote. "There's some kind of gun or shell exploding at all times. The first nite or two I couldn't sleep for the noise but now I don't notice them very much unless they come too close. Then we have a hole in the ground to dive into and I guess as long as we make it we'll be ok."

On July 2, he wrote to Gladys from a foxhole near the front. "At times it seems as tho we are past the front in enemy territory. We had quite a few big shells to fall among us and there was some scramble for holes by the ones that have been sleeping in the open. Several were close enough to throw dirt all down my back so from now on I think I'll dig into. It feels a lot safer that way anyhow. The biggest thing that bothers me is the noise. It's a thousand times worse than any movie you ever saw. The sky is practically filled with shells all the time during a barrage and the explosions are terrific. You don't get much sleep or rest while it lasts and you never know when it will start or how long it will last. Anyway, so far everything is all right."

He apologized to T.J. that he was unable to mark his eighth birthday, adding, "it was just impossible from here."

Missing his son's birthday again reminded Boyd that his boy was practically a stranger to him. "I don't suppose I'll hardly know T.J. when I get back," he wrote to Gladys. "He certainly will be a big boy compared to the last time I saw him. That's been three years you know." But that separation left him in a quandary, admitting he didn't know what he should do or try to do concerning T.J. He summed up his attitude in a letter to Gladys: "I have just tried not to think about it at all and hope that everything would eventually work out all right."

For Gladys and the rest of the family, envisioning the hell Boyd was going through in those foxholes was almost more than they could bear. Writing to her brother on August 9, 1944, she expressed that concern and tried to lift his spirits with news about T.J.

"We all cried when we read about the foxholes and I don't go to sleep at nite without praying for you & wishing you could be at home in your own nice bed I've got waiting for you—and your boy. As you can see from the pictures, he is getting quite big. He still enjoys the movies but hasn't been so much lately as there has been an epidemic of infantile paralysis in the area & Burlynn has kept him close. I spend the night out there about once a week & he comes with me once or twice. I took him to his first play not long ago—he wouldn't let any of us rest until he had gotten to see one. He said, 'But Gladys, I've never seen a play in my whole life!' I told him he wasn't very old yet and had plenty of time but just like his Life Rdg. said, 'What he wants, he wants now!' So we both enjoyed it very much—it was sort of a comedy. At the Casino right at the end of 14th, across from the Bama Stand, a summer stock company is playing, with a new show each week. He wanted very much to see Dracula when it was on, but we all refused to go with him to see that. There is a radio program called District Attorney that he enjoys very much—perhaps it was on while you were still here. He listens to every word & gets very impatient with anyone who says anything to distract him during the program. The man who lives next to them in Oceana has a garden & Thos. Jeff. is quite a pet around there—just loves to help plant & gather things. He would make an excellent farmer, of course, with his background. I've heard him tell people, 'When my Daddy comes back we're going to buy a farm & raise everything & have horses, too!'"

This also was the letter that Gladys first revealed that Edgar Cayce's health was beginning to fail. "Mr. Cayce has just gotten back from a ten-day visit to Tom Sugrue in Florida. He feels rested but is not well at all. I had planned a vacation in N.Y. but decided just to 'stay put' & get a few things done that I've been putting off for ages."

Gladys told Boyd that she had fixed up the living room with a sofa bed so it could be used as a bedroom at night. That was where she told Boyd he'd stay when he got home. T.J. slept there when he spent his nights with her. The sofa bed was next to one of her proudest possessions—her baby grand piano—even though she admitted she hadn't settled down to learn to play it yet.

Gladys did not talk about work very often in her letters, but in this one, she did. The article, "Miracle Man of Virginia Beach" by Marguerite Harmon Bro had just been published in the September 1943 issue of *Coronet Magazine*. The article drew national attention to Cayce's work, and as a result, the number of requests for readings increased significantly.

"If that *Coronet Magazine* will just run out of circulation I think we can settle down to some peace & calm once more," she wrote. "We had to put on an office force of about 10 people, all because of that article 'Miracle Man of Virginia Beach,' when—if it hadn't been for that—we might have had the same number of people working on something really important towards our research program. A lot of the confusion in the office has been caused by having to employ service men's wives who are constantly having to go off just after they've become familiar with a job. Gradually we are getting those, one by one, who can stay permanently & who are interested in the work itself & not just for pay. Those who don't belong will gradually weed themselves out. As the readings have said, those who don't belong can't stay in it & those who do belong can't get away from it. I certainly must belong!"

Gladys also told Boyd that Mrs. Cayce heard from Hugh Lynn, who was in France at the time. She hoped Boyd could meet up with him, but then added that would be almost a miracle if they did.

"He said that where he is it is comparatively safe— they went over in a convoy & the 1st sight on landing was an uncomfortable bunch of Germans in stockade," she wrote. "He said there wasn't room in the air for a German plane, where he was when he wrote."

As for Burlynn, Gladys informed her brother that his now ex-wife invited them to dinner. "You know how generous she is when she is in the mood for it," Gladys wrote. "She really has a lot of good qualities, as we very well know. Mr. Cayce had a dream about her several months ago—that she does have a lot of good in her & that we shouldn't condemn her even in our thoughts. Of course, that is what you always said—remember the lecture you gave me on it the last night you were here? By the way, I told her about your last letters & she was terribly concerned—said tell you she was thinking about you and hoping you'd come thru alright—that she wanted T.J. to be with you as much as you want him when you come back; said that you & she probably would never have made a go of it, but that you couldn't have a boy like Thos. Jeff. together & then not really 'care' about what happened to the other. You probably both would do any great big thing for the other that is in your power to do, but it is the little every day living that gets you. She doesn't do a thing without Rabbit's okay, & I guess he has helped her in some ways—he has kept her from drinking too much, Mae says, & that in itself is good. Not ever having known her father, I imagine Rabbit sort of fills a place like that with her, & she likes the material power that she thinks he has—which I feel is completely of the earth—earthy & with no lasting spiritual value at all. Still, we must live & learn. In the end perhaps she will learn a spiritual lesson from it all. We can only stand ready to help her when these other things, she puts so much trust in, fail."

By the end of August, Boyd was stationed somewhere in France, which may be why Gladys was hopeful he and Hugh Lynn would meet up somehow. Hugh Lynn had thoughtfully sent T.J. some English coins, which was a thrill for the boy to receive. This put the idea in Boyd's mind to send his son some French money to play with, as he didn't see much use for it in any other way.

"I'm glad H.L. thought to send him some coins or

something because I never would have given it a thought," he admitted to Gladys. "I never have cared anything for souvenirs and guess don't realize that other persons might. That makes me think—I could send him some French money if you think he'd like it. To me it's nothing but some very cheap paper. I'll keep on the outlook for something to send back, but where we are it's quite a job to even get a letter finally mailed much less a package. Too there are so few things we are allowed to send."

In addition to the French money, Boyd wanted to send T.J. a pair of wooden shoes, as everyone in Europe was wearing them. They were hard to come by but he finally found a pair and said he'd have to sandpaper them down and then have them painted before he could send them. Addressing their use in the United States, he wrote: "They will make good bookends or something if you wanted to keep them but I suppose he had rather play with them outside. Tell him the way the French make them fit us is to fill in all the empty space with straw. He'll probably have to use paper."

On October 9, Gladys wrote to Boyd that she was staying at the Cayce home, because " . . . he has been real sick and they need me—Mrs. Cayce isn't well either—not either one of them strong. They are still in Roanoke, as he is following treatment there, and they need someone here in the house to look after the rooms being rented. I rented my apartment but can get into it at any time—just in case you come back while it is still rented."

About a month before Mr. Cayce's death, Jeanne

Fitch, A.R.E. office secretary, began corresponding with Boyd. Jeanne was living in Gladys's home while Gladys was staying at the Cayce home. Since Gladys was so busy, she asked Jeanne to write to Boyd to acknowledge receipt of the $100 he sent home, as well as to bring him up-to-date on what was happening with Edgar.

Writing to Boyd on December 1, Jeanne told him that the Cayces had returned home a week earlier and everyone had pitched in to overhaul the house by moving beds and furniture and do a general cleaning. She said this, plus the office work, had created a "terribly confusing" atmosphere at the house. "Mr. Cayce isn't in very good condition," she wrote. "I hadn't seen him since August and when I saw him I had to get out of the room in a hurry. The left side of his body is paralyzed from the face down and he is so weak that he speaks with a whisper. He has managed to dictate a few personal letters to me, though. But it is rather hard to distinguish quite what he is saying, but between Gladys and me, we straighten it out. I'm sure that he will be alright, but it will take a long time to regain his strength. I feel so sorry about it all and have missed taking the readings so much. Gladys finally got someone to take them for her—but of course, she always went over them before sending them out. I have certainly enjoyed working with her and will never forget how patient she was with me at first . . . A crowd of the Norfolk group ladies are here this afternoon and Gladys is upstairs with them. I guess that she hasn't had a chance to even do one letter yet today and she has a desk full of them . . . She is certainly brave, patient, kind and understanding—at least, I always find her so! Sure wish that I had some of the stuff she is made of."

Jeanne told Boyd that Edgar Evans was home from Trinidad and had twenty days leave before having to report to Drew Field in Florida for further military orders. "It is so fortunate that he could get the leave right now when his father is so ill. They tried to see if Hugh Lynn could come home, but they said they needed him over there, so that's that! It is too bad you all can't come home, and I'll surely be happy when you can."

By December 29, Boyd still had not heard from Gladys. He wrote to her from England, letting her know he had been in the hospital for two months due to recurring back pain. The doctors were suggesting surgery, as there was nothing more they could do for him. He felt certain he would be re-classified and would have to work indoors but could not imagine what he was going to do. He said he would be away from home until 1950—a good six years away—and once again, asked Gladys to take care of T.J. for him.

No one could have known that within a week, Edgar Cayce would be dead and life for T.J., as he had come to know it, would be changed forever.

Chapter Nine
Educational Hodgepodge

The Cayce readings, family correspondence, and actions by those closest to T.J. Davis during Cayce's lifetime put him on a trajectory that gave him the best chance of fulfilling the destiny his life reading spread before him. Everything was in place for this child's soul to be nurtured, supported, and loved as he grew into maturity to achieve the purpose for which his soul's contract was written.

Considering the circumstances of his birth to parents whose karmic issues presented ongoing challenges for this child's soul to blossom, there were enough souls around him who were tasked with keeping T.J. on track for his highest and best. The ranks of individuals who had a positive influence on him were great indeed. Even so, he was legally the responsibility of Boyd and Burlynn Davis and subject to the decisions they made of their own free will.

There is no question that T.J. was adored by many of the men and women who were in the Cayce inner circle. They watched in amazement as he grew, looking for signs that the glory of his prior lifetimes would emerge once again and make a significant impact on an uncertain world. It was as if this child were seated alone on a train, itinerary in hand, headed to a destination where his combined karmic experiences and talents would be utilized to influence the world around him. Of this, Edgar Cayce was certain. So it was when that karmic train that little T.J. was on reached a crossroads, those who cared about him could do nothing but watch as a decision made by Burlynn diverted that train, setting it on a track that was leading to a very different destination than originally planned.

Edgar Cayce's influence on T.J.'s physical well-being was set in place for a lifetime of relative good health, which was fulfilled as he strictly followed the guidelines Cayce taught him. However, the area where Cayce's influence fell on deaf ears had to do with T.J.'s education—the one area about his life that T.J. has the most bitterness about today. It is here that he said his parents "truly let me down."

Cayce was adamant about how important this aspect of T.J.'s development would be and gave very specific instructions, saying: " . . . there should be the correct guidance and training in his formative years" (1208-1, T20).

Things started out on the right foot, as there are numerous notations in his file about how much T.J. loved school. In a letter dated September 16, 1940, Cayce described T.J.'s excitement at the thought of starting school. "...and then—Miss Davis' nephew who is with us and has been all summer starts to kindergarten this morning—he is all a titter, and am sure will keep the lady [Miss Lillian Barclay] who is taking on the work of training him a worse case of the same."

In early 1942 there was correspondence between Edgar Cayce and Beulah Hepburn Emmet about educational opportunities for T.J. at her new school, called the High Mowing School, in Wilton, New Hampshire. A longtime follower of the writings of the Austrian philosopher and scientist Rudolf Steiner, Mrs. Emmet founded a school inspired by Steiner's revolutionary educational philosophies. It was the first Waldorf high school to be founded in North America, and today it remains the only Waldorf boarding school in North America.

Cayce had given Mrs. Emmet a life reading on April 20, 1940, telling her that one of her previous lifetimes was in Greece where she was involved " . . . in the artistic development of individuals, through its associations and activities in the Grecian land and the Grecian thought, are a part of the entity…" (2174-1, T31). He also told her she was in Atlantis at the time of the great exodus, where she " . . . held to the principles of the Law of One" (2174-1, T50). Both of these lives would have placed her in the same time period as T.J.'s sojourns as Alexander in Greece, and Sululon in Atlantis. This would explain Cayce's keen interest in her teaching T.J., as the two souls would have resumed a relationship they had had nearly two thousand years earlier.

So it was that Cayce wrote to Mrs. Emmet on March 21, 1942, congratulating her on the opening of the school, saying it would "do a world of good and that is what is needed at this time, to prepare the young folks to take hold of the problems that this present unpleasantness is producing meeting them in the way as to bring each person as well as the country as a whole the need and the necessity to getting closer to GOD."

In May 1942, Mrs. Emmet wrote to Edgar and asked if he wanted to send T.J. to her then, informing him that she could take him any time. Cayce said he would talk it over with her when she came to visit, adding: " . . . been some changes there but there is needed such training now for him more than ever would be a wonderful experiment - and I believe his salvation."

A few weeks after T.J.'s sixth birthday, Cayce gave a reading on the boy's behalf concerning his schooling. The reading was done at Boyd and Burlynn's request. T.J. was there, along with Gertrude, Burlynn, and Gladys. The question they asked was, considering his age and surroundings, and those at that school, would it be a good idea for him to attend that school. Cayce's Source answered:

> . . . those possibilities and probabilities as may be in the experience of this entity in this material sojourn, under the direction or development *in* that direction which has been indicated.

As we find, then, the conditions that are to be considered are the environs of the school, the developments and the aims and purposes of those who direct same, and the ability of those directing same to interpret - in mental and material ways - those suggestions which have been given, which may be given, respecting the unfoldment of this body-mind.

For, as we find, those abilities, those tendencies, those urges that have been indicated for this entity *are* apparent, if there will be the correct analysis of this unfolding mind.

As to the ability, as to the place, as to the environ, - this as we find would be as near ideal as might well be imagined. And thus this is the *correct* age, if there is to be the consideration of the body-mind itself.

But this should not be that as of an experiment, rather as of a fact. Thus those that are interested should lend every help possible. For, there will be the proper consideration given by those in authority in this particular school, in this particular environ.

If there is an analysis of those that were contemporaries with the entity, that were speakers from that portion of the country, we will understand why there is the outward expression with the entity in the desire to go there.

This also should be considered by those as they enable the entity to form its ideas, its ideals: *do keep the ideal in the spiritual import. Do give the opportunity for self-unfoldment*; not self-indulgence, to be sure - for this is as a problem in the experience of the entity.

Not that there will not be days when the entity may be, for the moment, unhappy - and would make those who are responsible feel as if possibly it would be a temptation to change the environs. But give the entity this opportunity. Lend self, even make sacrifices for it. Not only is it that the entity may have the opportunity for the better expression, but *think what the entity may mean, can mean, to so many others*! (1208-18, T2–9).

In short, the reading was stating it was a good idea, considering that T.J. was already having trouble in public school. Cayce advised that T.J. be enrolled that September and that he stay at the school until he was ready for college. There was a sense of urgency conveyed in this reading, as it ended with a warning, "This is an opportunity - don't let it pass - for his sake" (1208-18, T15).

T.J. happily anticipated the adventure that awaited him. Quoting one of his famous sayings, Gladys told T.J.'s father, "The other night, soon after getting back from Ohio, he was telling me about a new pencil box Ruby had given him. He said, 'You know, Gladys, I'm going to take it to school with me. When I go to school I'm going to study Geoggity (geography).'"

On August 28, 1942, about a month before T.J. was slated to leave, Gladys wrote to her brother asking if he could get a long enough leave to come to Virginia Beach to see T.J. before he left for school. It was apparent she had every expectation that little T.J. would be going to New Hampshire very shortly.

"He will probably leave here on the 23rd, or something like that. I plan to have him back here for Xmas," she wrote. "Burlynn mentioned that she might go up and get him then. Mrs. Emmet could probably bring him to N.Y. He is going to be quite a traveled little boy for his age. I believe the other Thomas Jefferson went to boarding school at six—I know he was quite young, and at fourteen was taking care of his mother and sisters."

Two weeks later Gladys wrote to Mrs. Emmet, detailing plans for their arrival.

"Dear Mrs. Emmet:
"We have arranged our appointments so that I can come up and bring T.J., as his mother can't get off. So I plan to take the Pennsylvania train leaving for New York from here on Friday night the 18th, and get to Boston around

1:10 on Saturday. Is this alright, and could I get a bus to Wilton from Boston or will somebody have to meet me? Please let me know about this, and if you do have to meet me would Saturday be alright—or should I plan to arrive in Boston on Sunday? I know you are too busy to be bothered with all these details, but I want to get there at the best time for all concerned. It is going to mean a lot to me to come with him this first time, and to see him established, also to see all of you *and* the school. I have had a great feeling of release since the Reading said what it did about High Mowing being the ideal place for him. I do hope his parents will prove worthy of this great opportunity, by doing their part—or at least the part that is left them, since I feel that they have let slide their most wonderful part, long ago. But, who am I to question them—and perhaps it is all for the best. I assure you I'll do everything I can to keep his parents in line with what the Reading says . . . Love, and appreciation. Gladys.

"P.S. T.J. still talks enthusiastically about coming. Our public schools started here today, but he is not the least bit concerned. He just loves to tell people that he is going to *New Hampshire* to school. All our Norfolk people, who heard you speak at the Congress, are thrilled at this opportunity for T.J."

Beulah Emmet answered the letter four days later with travel and accommodation arrangements and acknowledging their arrival.

But then, rather abruptly, Burlynn refused to send him. Gladys made a notation in T.J.'s file that read, "The mother changed her mind - did not want him to be so far away from her. He did not go to the school."

On September 15, Cayce wrote to Mrs. Emmet explaining the situation. "Now about [T.J.]. Guess Miss [Gladys] has written you - His mother has gone back on everything she said, and is not willing for him to leave so that is that. Why some things aren't different and why some people do as they do can't ever say - but who am I to judge."

In another letter, he went further and expressed his disappointment. "[T.J.'s] mother got cold feet, said she couldn't bear to think of his being so far away from her when he was so young. Hard to say what is what - just hope she never regrets it. Am disappointed, yet not surprised, but she had been so willing when I made arrangements. Do not know what happened to her."

Mrs. Emmet replied: "It is *tragic* that [T.J.] is not with us. Is there someway in which his mother could *see* it. How can a person know what it is like unless they see it? Even we who should have known did not realize what it was going to be. He will come through sometime."

To which Mr. Cayce responded, "I could never put into words how disappointed I was that [T.J.] didn't start off with you there, and the less I say about those things as caused the change in the attitude of the mother possibly will be better, but the father [391] is now in England, while true they are separated, yet that fact possibly had much to do with her decision of not sending him at this time. Maybe he will come just hope so for his sake."

T.J. said he has had many turning points in his life—when a decision by those who were caring for him took him down one path or the other—but this incident with the High Mowing School was the most pivotal event in his life and one he continues to regret.

"Can you imagine having the privilege of getting personal counseling from Edgar Cayce about a soul he loved dearly and then ignoring it?" he asked. "The statement about my mother not wanting me to be so far away from her just boggles my mind. My mother was so unstable that I was sent back and forth between her and the Cayces as if I were a ping-pong ball. She never lived in any one place for any length of time. When she pulled me away from the Cayces, it wasn't for very long— perhaps a month or two—but then I'd end up in another school—sometimes two or three times in one year. I'd attend school in Virginia Beach and the next thing I know, I'm back in school in Ohio."

Right after the reading about High Mowing School, T.J. was going to public school in Virginia Beach and living with Gladys. Despite the disappointment at not going away to school, T.J. still maintained his enthusiasm for learning, as Gladys shared in an October 7, 1942, letter to her brother Burt.

"Yesterday morning he came running upstairs telling me it was time to get up, as he had to go to school right away or he would be late. I said, 'Run down and ask

Mama what time it is.' He said, 'Gladys, it's those round things—you know, like this!' And he made a sign with his two thumbs and forefingers like this, meaning eight o'clock."

According to a note Gladys made in his file, at that point, he "still brought home interesting drawings which the teacher said showed 'actions.' [1922] says he is real good in school and minds her nicely."

In a letter to Boyd dated October 17, 1942, Gladys wrote: "We have had rain for a whole week now. It is raining and cloudy again today, and Thos. Jeff. said a minute ago, 'I wish I was going to school today.' Madeline says he is real good in school, and minds her nicely. The first grade was so large that the class was divided, and Madeline kept him in her room. His books came to $2.72. Can you imagine that? He is very thrilled at having a book bag, and you should see him marching off to school so big. We see him across the boulevard, then he comes to the office in the afternoon, walking the path to 16th St. with the other children and around by Miss Barclay's— with little Joe Smithson who lives down the street."

Shortly after that date (2/4/43) T.J. changed schools. A letter from Gladys to the War Department, Office of Dependency Benefits, stated he was living with Burlynn at the Oceana Restaurant in Oceana. His first-grade teacher, Mrs. Lucy M. Hatchett, wrote on his June 9 report card that he annoyed others in class, made unnecessary noise, was prompt in work habits and response to direction. His grades were a B in reading, language, physical education, music, and drawing; C in writing; and D in arithmetic.

Even though it looked as though T.J. would never attend High Mowing School, Beulah Emmet continued to hold out hope that things would turn around. In a letter to Edgar Cayce on May 1, 1943, she wrote: "My love to you all [including [T.J.]. I wonder if I will ever have him. We have had to give up our lower grades for next year because of the demand for space (beds) in the upper grades. That is only temporary I know. I wonder if that would have happened if he had come."

Several days later, Edgar wrote back, sharing Beulah's hope that she would have an opportunity to educate T.J. "Hope yet it will be possible for you to have [T.J.] for some part of his training at least," he wrote.

By October 1943, T.J. was back with Gladys and in public school in Virginia Beach. In 1944 and 1945 Gladys reported that he was with Burlynn most of the time, but that he was switched from one school to another, staying a month or so in a public school and then switched to a private school for a few months, and so on.

In 1947 she reported that T.J. had changed schools three times that year, and that his general standing was "D." In June 1947, T.J.'s teacher at William Rainey Harper School noted that he needed to improve in all subjects and that he would need additional time to complete the work of the upper elementary levels. His teacher, Easter Adams, commented: "The work is new for Thomas and so I think he will have a much better foundation if he repeats this grade. He is careless and hasn't made the most of his time. I'm sure he will do better."

Things did not seem to improve when he returned to school. On October 20, 1947, he wrote to his mother, "I was making airplanes in school while I was supposed to be studying."

A week later his teacher, Miss Orlan M. Mull, sent home his report card with a notation that he needed to improve his self-control, promptness, and self-reliance. "T.J. doesn't seem to be able to apply himself or try to keep busy," she noted. "I would be happy to see him really put forth the effort to be cooperative in the classroom and study. I am sure that he can do his work. There are (43) forty-three in the class and not much time for individual attention and no time for *play*."

In October 1948, Gladys reported that T.J. received an "A" (in yet another school) for a map of South America he drew, colored, and marked. He had a paper route that year and saved his money. It was the only school year in which he was allowed to stay put and finish the year out at the same school.

Just before he turned seventeen, Gladys wrote that T.J.'s teacher reported he had not been turning in his assignments and suggested it was because of girl trouble. Later she reported that he failed English and was supposed to go to summer school, but instead ran away with a friend to Florida.

"The truth is, there were some kids in school who were famous for bullying other students," T.J. clarified.

"They had threatened to beat me up so I was looking for a way to escape. My friend Jimmy's father owned a chicken ranch in Florida, so I decided to hitchhike down there to see if I could get a job. Jimmy and I jumped on a train and landed in a car that was full of coal dust. When the train stopped, we thought we were in Florida, but we actually were in a tiny town in South Carolina. We were filthy from the coal dust, so I imagine we looked like trouble. Jimmy only had $3 on him and I had no money whatsoever. He gave me the money and told me to go into the five and dime and get us some food, but instead I bought myself some clean socks. Needless to say, Jimmy was not happy about that. The police stopped us because there was a missing persons report on the two of us. Jimmy was sent on to Florida to be with his dad and I returned to Virginia. The bullies did not bother me after that."

This wasn't the last time he got into trouble. Gladys noted in his file that T.J. and his friend "got into trouble on account of 'borrowing' things and not returning them. They escaped punishment only because of being under age, and because of the help of friends."

T.J. challenged the interpretation of that note as meaning he got into trouble for stealing. "That's not exactly true," he stated. "When I was around seventeen, I was working at a local laundry/dry cleaner in Virginia Beach and was in charge of driving the company van to deliver clothes. Steven, one of the other guys working there, was a real smart aleck and talked me into taking the van so we could drive to Florida. Like my previous trip to Florida, I didn't have any money on me and neither did my companion. Since we only had so much gas in the van, we didn't get any further than Suffolk and then had to turn around. The owner of the dry cleaning place was mad that we 'borrowed' the van, but even so, he didn't fire me. I was close to his daughter and spent a lot of time with his family, so he did not equate my 'borrowing' the van as stealing it."

T.J. does admit he got into trouble while in high school, but he never thought it was any more or any less than what other teenage boys did during those years. Nonetheless, those were rough years. He started out with a lot of promise and great hope and ended up running away. During his entire academic life, he was nothing more than a vagabond student who, like his mother, never stayed in any one place for any length of time.

"What irritates me the most about this is if I had such a spectacular purpose and ability to do what Mr. Cayce said I would do, why didn't anyone help me achieve that?" he questioned. "If my education was a key factor in my ability to fulfill that destiny, why did everyone stand idly by and allow my mother—an alcoholic who did not want me in the first place—to make such life-changing decisions on my behalf? I don't mean to come across as the classic victim and give the impression that I feel sorry for myself. It just never made sense to me and even now I don't understand what happened. Even if they treated me like a business, someone would have said, 'Well, look, let's help him follow the plan that Mr. Cayce set out for him.' Who knows how different my life would have been had that happened."

Chapter Ten

Cayce's Passing

Unless you have experienced the sorrow
of being away from home, lonely and
confused as to what to do, spiritually,
mentally, materially, you cannot know
what a hunger it creates.
—Edgar Cayce, "Coming Home"
Christmas Message, December 1944

This beginning sentence of Edgar's Christmas Message, written just weeks before he died, would aptly describe T.J.'s life once Edgar was gone. In the years following Cayce's death, T.J. did indeed experience the sorrow of being away from the home he shared with his mentor; he was lonely for the company of Eddie Cay-kee, and certainly, as a child looking for guidance where there was none, he was definitely "confused as to what to do." The hunger that created has stayed with him for an entire lifetime and his actions—whether one agrees with them or not—have been greatly influenced by that sense of being a lost soul without an understanding of how to accomplish the great challenge before him.

T.J. measures his world in terms of before and after Edgar died. Before Cayce passed on, T.J.'s childhood was the complete opposite of what other children his age were experiencing in their homes, living in a house full of people who were there because they were on a spiritual journey. All those folks who patted him on the head every day knew his life reading and he knew theirs. It was no accident that they were together during those formative years.

But just before Mr. Cayce died, T.J. said the atmosphere around the A.R.E. changed. He sensed that Mr. Cayce wasn't going to have enough time to do what he needed to do. His concern was warranted, as Edgar Cayce died on January 3, 1945, at 7:15 p.m. The shock of his passing brought on unbelievable grief for those who knew him, and even on those who did not. Thomas Sugrue, writing for the A.R.E. Bulletin, composed an editorial about Cayce, attesting to the depth of despair everyone close to Cayce felt at his untimely passing.

"As this is written the shock of his passing is so deep that even the most glib tongues are stilled," Sugrue wrote. "Once a person came to know Edgar Cayce, he thereafter could not imagine a world without him, without his readings, without his personality, his friendliness, his simple and complete Christianity."

Being unable to imagine a world without Cayce was especially difficult for eight-year-old Thomas

Jefferson Davis.

"When Mr. Cayce died, I didn't know what to do," T.J. admitted. "The life I knew just stopped, rather abruptly. I was terrified. I didn't know what to think or what to do and my future was no longer as sure as it had been when Mr. Cayce was there as my guardian and my mentor. How was I to know at that young age that no matter what Mr. Cayce may have wanted, with him gone, his plan would be ignored? I later learned that much of what he wanted—besides my continued upbringing in the A.R.E.—would be ignored."

In the months after Cayce's death, T.J. sensed that the A.R.E. he had come to know was beginning to disappear.

"People were scurrying around," he said. "No one knew what to do because he was the common denominator that held everything together. *He* was the one. That's what it was all about—what Mr. Cayce could do and how he could help people. Gladys had all she could do to hang on and keep the place rolling. She was all over the place because she knew she had to save the readings. This is when I realized what Mr. Cayce meant when he was dying and told me things weren't working out as he planned. Here I had this reading where everybody there thought I was going to save the world and do all these wonderful things, but once Mr. Cayce was gone, it felt as though not only did he leave me, but everyone else left me to fend on my own as well. At that point I had no one to live with. My mother was still down the street so Gladys turned me back over to her, but my mother still couldn't handle being a parent. She would farm me off to other relatives and send money so they would take care of me."

T.J. had an aunt and cousin in Ohio, and he was put on a bus to live with them. From there he went to live with his grandmother in Adams County, Ohio. When she died, T.J. moved in with his aunt Beatrice, uncle George, and their family. While he loved his uncle, who became a father figure for him, T.J.'s stay there was temporary. With Burlynn running out of relatives capable of taking care of T.J., she hired a woman in town who let the boy stay with her. In a short time, he went from living in the loving household of the Cayce family, then to various relatives, and finally living with complete strangers.

T.J. said when he thinks of Mr. Cayce passing before he had the chance to receive that second life reading, he realizes how important that must have been to both of them because of the way he received the first reading.

"I was just a few days old when I got that life reading," he said. "He knew what was coming up and he wanted to make sure I was prepared. He spent hours talking to me about the creation story and about past lifetimes and how I can pull from different life aspects into this life if I needed to. He was teaching me how to write my resume where I would spell out what I had to offer the world.

"For the first eight and one-half years of my life, I lived in a house that was full of karmic relationships, some of which resulted in having people in power that did not like me very much. My life—with all that enormous potential that Mr. Cayce said was ahead of me—went from applause to yawn. When he was alive, I looked forward to receiving that second life reading on my thirteenth birthday because I knew whatever he would tell me would be exciting and set the foundation for the work I would be doing. He already said I was very capable of doing all he had predicted, but with him gone, I wondered how was I supposed to be all he said I could be now?"

As a child T.J.'s thoughts started to shift as he pondered the ramifications of Mr. Cayce's premature demise. He saw himself in a strange way, feeling at times as though he was from another planet. He tried to focus on basketball and baseball and other "normal" childhood interests, but all he could think about was Atlantis is going to rise. He thought by the time he reached fifty it wouldn't matter because everything would be gone.

"And I was supposed to save the world?" he asked sarcastically. "It was totally overwhelming. To be honest, if it hadn't been for Mr. Cayce and all the mystical things that went on around us, I would have shoved this away a long time ago. Knowing how different my life was from anyone else's, I learned to keep my mouth shut, even though my self-imposed silence bothered me on a deep soul level."

PART TWO

Memories and Observations

Chapter Eleven
"A Blessed Darling"

Gertrude Cayce with T.J., August 1939. (ECF#1061)

In part 1 of this narrative, we have explored the journey from T.J.'s conception through his sometimes-tumultuous childhood through the lens of those closest to him. The documentation found in the readings and in the archives of the Edgar Cayce Foundation has enabled his family and others who were center stage during these formative years to share their story in their own voice. We have watched as his family, who had the advantage of the Cayce readings as a guidepost on how to raise this precious boy, grappled with the challenges of their own karmic issues. The decisions that were made along the way were influenced by their experiences during these post-Depression years and with the country being involved in a world war, not to mention their own struggles with alcohol, gambling, and scarcity of work opportunities.

Now in part 2, the narrative focuses on how T.J., as an adult, remembers the years he spent in the Cayce household. It is important to keep in mind that he is talking as a man in his seventies looking back some sixty-odd years. Even though this much time has passed, his version will give you a feel for what he was going through.

What makes T.J. so special is the fact that equally special people surrounded him. He had the potential to fulfill a promise only if others could keep their promise. The first part of the book brings to light why they couldn't keep those promises in the hope that the reader would feel some compassion for those souls charged with his upbringing. So much was riding on their decisions—his education, a stable home life—all of that was proposed to the parents via the readings. People around him were trying to compensate for what he wasn't getting from his parents in the world he lived in. He was already wounded. This last part of the book will provide insights into how that wounded soul reacted in the aftermath.

Before addressing the magnitude of the impact the loss of Edgar Cayce had on T.J.'s life, it's important to go back and explore in more detail what T.J.'s daily life was like living with the Cayces. His life has been portrayed from his family's viewpoint, but how did this little boy, so full of promise, see the world around him?

While it is true that T.J. was not in Virginia Beach on a consistent basis, when he was at the Cayce compound, he and Edgar spent a lot of time together. It is undeniable that the two formed an enormous bond—one that had implications that few failed to see even though Edgar did all he could to convince those around him about the importance of this young soul.

So, what was it like to be a child living in the Cayce household? Early in T.J.'s life, he was surrounded almost exclusively by the adults who lived and worked at the A.R.E. He had few, if any, companions his age, and he often vocalized that complaint to Edgar, asking where were all the kids?

"He tried to placate me by saying, 'Well, maybe they'll show up sooner or later,'" T.J. recalled. "'You're with me now, so let's just leave it like that.' And we did."

Still, Cayce was wrapped up in his work most of the time, and T.J. came to cherish the time they did spend together.

"It wasn't as if he worked for IBM and had a nine-to-five job where he'd come home and want a drink and listen to the stereo," T.J. said. "He was more like a doctor who always was on call because at any moment, someone would need something. His life revolved around the readings. Consequently, he didn't have much of a social life. A normal day for us was to get up, go out and work in the garden for a while, watering and weeding the plants. Then he'd ask me if I wanted to fish and I'd always say yes. We'd go out to the lake and then come back and he'd give a reading. By then it was dinnertime."

T.J. said that although Edgar was very busy, there always was time for the two of them to do things like go to the barbershop or walk on the beach.

"I don't know what he did with other people," T.J. said, "but I know that we both liked to do the same things, like going to the movies. He usually picked science fiction or movies about dinosaurs that scared me, so I would hide in my seat the whole time and not enjoy the film at all. But that didn't matter. I was with him and that's all I cared about."

Although T.J. went to church services with the Cayces quite often, he admitted that he didn't like attending Sunday school. He used to sneak into the bathroom and climb out the window.

"It wasn't that I didn't like church," he explained. "It was just that all my friends from school were there. Because of my relationship with Mr. Cayce, many of those kids bullied me relentlessly. They'd say, 'Here comes the weird kid.' To avoid their ridicule, I pretty much stayed to myself. I'd go down to the beach and wait for him to finish."

T.J. described Edgar as being a good Sunday school teacher who taught a Bible class at the First Presbyterian Church. He never understood why Edgar stopped teaching, but surmised it may have had to do with his changing beliefs.

"He was sincere in his beliefs, but his interpretation of the Bible was different than the others in that church," T.J. said. "We read the Bible together quite a bit. He read it every day and part of my job was to listen. Much of it I found boring, but he found a way to make it interesting in a way no one else could. That's because he actually knew many of the people in the Bible. I'd often hear him say: 'I remember him.' A lot of them were the Essenes, the people who paved the way for Christ to come."

Although T.J. was close to Edgar, he never developed a close relationship with Mrs. Cayce, whom he called Muddie Cay-kee. There is not much written about the two of them, but Gladys noted that Edgar Cayce wrote that his wife was crazy about T.J. Even though T.J. did not remember that being the case, he surmised there must have been some affection for him on her part.

Gertrude was curious about their past-life relationship, though. In a reading she asked, "Was I associated with Alexander the Great, now [little [1208]], and how? ... What are the urges to be met in the present, for our mutual development?" (538-59, T20).

Cayce's Source told her that the role she should play in his life was "As a nurse, or as a caretaker, and governing a part of the educational forces as became a part of the influence under the students of, or contemporaries with, the father of the entity." He acknowledged that she did, indeed, fill the role of nurse and caretaker.

"I only have a few vivid memories of Mrs. Cayce," T.J. said. "One is when Mr. Cayce and I came off the pier, I'd come into the house complaining about how short I was. In response, Mrs. Cayce would have me stand against the kitchen door and mark off how tall I had grown since the last time she measured me. That was exciting, but that door had some unpleasant memories for me as well. Mr. Cayce sometimes liked to play dentist. If I had a loose tooth, he'd tie a string on the tooth and the other end to the door and he'd tell me to count to five and there went my tooth!"

His other clear memory of Mrs. Cayce was when he would try to help in the kitchen. T.J. was interested in cooking but wasn't very good at it, so Gertrude had him do other chores, usually washing dishes or sweeping the floor. T.J. described Gertrude as friendly and always nice to him, yet at the same time strict.

"I could tell she was concerned about Mr. Cayce all the time," he said. "When I think back I can see her, but she pretty much stayed out of the picture as far as I was concerned. She and I just did not do anything together. Everything was built around Mr. Cayce. His aura was so huge and he was so unusual, that it would not have mattered whom he was married to. Everything he did preoccupied our thoughts."

Other memories T.J. had of being with the Cayces occurred at mealtime when they would all gather around the table.

"When I was very young, I was the only one who was allowed to have bacon," he said. "Mr. Cayce said that crisp bacon in small portions was acceptable, but Mrs. Cayce seldom made it—except for me. The reason I was the exception was a result of information contained in one of my readings as a way to fight off the effects of the alcohol I had ingested in my mother's womb."

When he was around fourteen months old, Cayce gave a health reading for T.J. in which he said: "We find that of a morning crisp bacon, well mashed, taken at the time the yolk of egg is given, would be most satisfying as well as agreeing with the digestive forces of the body" (1208-8, T4).

He addressed it again six months later: "Then in the foods we would keep the citrus fruit juices, vegetables; very crisp bacon with the yolk of an egg…" (1208-12, T11).

"I knew Mr. Cayce loved bacon and that he was watching me, so whenever I would eat it, knowing he could read my mind, I just kept thinking about how much I loved bacon!" T.J. laughed.

T.J. said that after what he shared about bacon, it might be hard for some people to believe that Cayce occasionally snuck bacon out to the pier.

"We'd get up at 4:30 in the morning and he would cook bacon while everyone was asleep and then put it in my lunch box," T.J. recalled. "I'm not sure how no one managed to smell the bacon cooking, but it remained our little secret. We would walk out to the pier and he would eat the bacon with a smile, as if it were our private joke. After all, who was going to see him on the pier eating bacon at that time of the morning? So even though when I grew older he told me a million times not to eat bacon, when I see bacon in the grocery store today I think of him out on that pier, munching on a crisp bacon strip with much relish."

T.J. said Edgar had a bamboo pole and used a cork, hook, and worms to fish. He kept a basket on the pier in which to store the fish.

"He'd catch a dozen or so in what seemed like the blink of an eye," T.J. said. "I never caught many fish, but it didn't matter to me. I liked to sit out there with him because he would talk to me—not as if I were a child but as if I were ageless, because we were ageless. We had done so many things together over many lifetimes. When we talked it wasn't—'oh boy we had a good time last Saturday.' It was more like—'Do you remember when we were in the pyramids and we had trouble trying to levitate those stones?' As we had this conversation, in my head I would be watching him put the pyramids together."

Looking back T.J. said he was amazed that Mr. Cayce spent as much time with him as he did. In fact,

T.J. was surprised that during those early days that anyone had time for him at all. "Everyone was working hard to build the A.R.E.," he said. "Gladys was busy transcribing the readings and working in the vault. Mae St. Clair was working on something else. Many times, just to give me something to do, they would let me run the mimeograph machine. That's what I did for entertainment."

Gladys, who said T.J. "tickles me to death" with some of the things the three-year-old would say, told her mother in a letter written July 25, 1939: "He is really recreation for me, if I can just find the time to listen to him and play with him, instead of having to try to keep him occupied while I work."

When T.J. was six, Gladys described his helpfulness in the office. In a letter to her brother on August 28, 1942, she wrote: "The other day Thos. Jeff was playing with a lot of old papers, sheets left over from using the mimeograph, and some old maps that he has had a long time. I noticed that he had a stack of these sheets with the folded map over the end of it, just like he has seen our stacks of letters waiting to be folded and put in the envelope. I said, 'What have you been doing, getting out some letters?' 'Yes,' he answered, 'I had to get out some imitations for the army.' He meant invitations. He has seen Miss Kerfoot, the recreational worker here with Hugh Lynn, get out cards, etc., inviting girls to dances for the soldiers."

In that same letter, she talked about how hospitable T.J. was. "Everyone who comes by the house he invites to come in and stay with us, or to eat with us."

T.J. recalled that Edgar liked to give readings as soon as the sun came up. That created a problem for the boy because he didn't have a bedroom of his own. At some point, every bedroom in the house was spoken for so Edgar let T.J. sleep in his office.

"My bed was the couch he used when giving readings," T.J. said. "If he didn't have to give a reading that morning, which was unusual, I would go outside. I'd hang around his window and throw rocks at it to get him to go out so we could go fishing. But if he was going to do a reading that morning, I'd have to get up at 5:30 or 6:00 a.m. On those days I was sent into the library, which was in the middle of the house. The library had a long table, a wall full of books and a few wooden chairs that weren't very comfortable."

Despite having a library full of books, T.J. claims he never saw Edgar studying them. Considering that the majority of the readings concerned health issues, the fact that he did not open a medical book made an impression on the young boy.

"He didn't even graduate from middle school, but still he was a very smart man," T.J. said. "I don't care if you went to Harvard or Oxford, if somebody is going to ask you a question about something that only a handful of people know and you give a correct answer, that's smart. And that's what Mr. Cayce did."

As a child T.J. spent a lot of time with Gladys while she worked in the office. "The vault was a big deal," he said. "Gladys always was working there and in a way, so was I because while she was working, I'd curl up in the vault and sleep on the bundles of mail near the readings. I'd just go in there and lie down. Mr. Cayce thought it was funny in a way and teased me, saying I could sleep on them all I wanted but I would never know what was in them the way he did."

As anyone who has read the Cayce readings can attest, understanding the language can be challenging. When Edgar was alive, T.J. had no problem understanding the readings, saying he found them "pretty interesting" because of the way Cayce interacted with him. Consequently, reading them felt the same as if Edgar were talking to him.

"Someone gave him a question and he answered it," T.J. said. "The readings were like an extension course, or added credit, of what I got from the tutoring I received when he and I were together. At times it felt that I was literally hooked up to the readings and that they were coming into my brain so I could draw on them at some future time. This was why whenever Mr. Cayce talked to me about things like Atlantis, fairies and elementals, the pyramids being erected in Egypt, etc., I actually would see what he was talking about. Because of that, I could engage in an adult conversation with him on those topics."

Gladys wrote a letter to her mother on July 25, 1939, when T.J. was just three years of age that attested to his fascination with the readings. "Now here's a very peculiar thing about him: He's just as active all day long as he can be, never still a minute. You remember how quick he is, and never sits still to even play with one thing very long at a time. But he just *loves* to 'sit in' and listen to the Readings. He'll sit through a long Reading, sometimes thirty or forty minutes, in one chair, just as quietly as you would in church. Now isn't that queer? And whenever we tell him we're going to take a Reading, he wants to come right in. It seems queer that he would *want* to sit quietly like that and listen to something when he doesn't even understand the words probably."

As T.J. grew older, he not only read all the readings but every book that was in the Cayce library. Even if he didn't like the book, he would read it. Books containing illustrations especially mesmerized him. One such book by Manly Palmer Hall fed his interest in art.

When he wasn't reading, T.J. spent a lot of time drawing and making copies of just about everything. This skill manifested early as verified by a notation in his file when he was just two. "Mother reported that [T.J.] loved to draw pictures and to draw figures which simulated handwriting."

Just before his fifth birthday, his mother wrote that his drawing skills extended to entertaining others. "Sunday [T.J.] and I stayed for church and he amused all the kids around us (grown ups too) by drawing these queer little figures. It's amazing the things he does. I've saved some of them that are really good, and the ideas are all his own."

T.J. credits those early years that he spent in

the Cayce library as starting his lifelong love of books, although Gladys made a notation in his file that until 1963 he hadn't been known to complete the reading of a book. Suddenly he was sitting up all hours of the night to paint and/or read. Today he reads on average one book a day and has pretty much exhausted the books in the local library. He is thankful for the abundance of used bookstores in Charlottesville.

As a child, T.J. also showed a talent for music. In a letter Gladys wrote on January 19, 1939, she noted: "One of our group members in Norfolk who makes violins is going to make a small one for him and start teaching him to play. So we will soon find out whether he has brought over any of his musical ability in that direction."

That latter comment was a direct reference to the Jefferson lifetime. Jefferson's musical ability is well documented. He began taking violin lessons as a young boy and enjoyed playing that instrument well into his old age.

Those early years in the Cayce household were idyllic for young T.J. Those who knew him as a child described him with great affection.

In a postcard that Lydia Schrader sent to Gladys on December 10, 1939, when T.J. was three and a half years old, she said she had seen T.J. and his mother, describing T.J. as "a blessed darling."

When he wasn't living at the Beach, his presence was sorely missed and whenever he returned, Gladys, being the doting aunt that she was, proclaimed, "He gets cuter all the time."

Since, as a preschooler, T.J. had few friends his own age, he had little chance to develop his social skills with his peers. On those rare occasions when he did have an interaction with another child, Gladys took note of it and left behind her observations. In an August 13, 1939, letter to her mother, she wrote: "At Mr. Ellington's he played with the little boy next door, named Raymond, who is about his age. One morning Raymond's mother had taken him to see his grandmother, so he didn't come over to play as usual. Thos. Jeff. kept wondering about Raymond and why he didn't come, and finally he said to me, 'Gladys, go find me with Raymond,' meaning, 'go with me to find Raymond.'"

Gladys put a notation in T.J.'s file on August 27, 1940, discussing his bossiness around other children. She wrote, "The other day little Roddey Miller from N.C. was here to play with him and brought his rifle. Thos. Jeff. has had about three rifles during the summer and has lost them all; consequently, he wanted to play with Roddey's rifle at once. However, Roddey being four years old and having a mind of his own wouldn't let him have it. Of course, Thos. Jeff. is a year older than Jobie and Jerry, and usually bosses them around to a certain extent, - at least, he plans the games and they follow suit."

Besides bossing around the other children, T.J. could be very loud at times. In that same note, Gladys wrote: "The day we were expecting the Millers to come, Thos. Jeff. woke up thinking about Roddey's arrival and planning for it and talking about it. He was talking about what we would do, and after a while he asked me, 'Gladys, can we yell?' Sometimes he just yells out without any apparent reason, though he must have one, and it might be at the most inconvenient time; so we had been talking to him about being a nice boy and not yelling in the house. So he thought that with Roddey coming he might have the special privilege of yelling again."

His bossiness and yelling apparently did not limit itself to playing with his friends. In that same notation, Gladys said T.J.'s bossiness extended to Mr. Cayce as well. "Early this morning I heard him downstairs yelling to Mr. C., 'Eddie Cakie, you do so and so; I'll tell Gladys on you and she'll come right down here and spank you!'"

While he could be stubborn, T.J. was definitely a charmer, even at the age of three. In a letter to her mother on August 13, 1939, Gladys wrote: "The other day I was trying to get him to do something he didn't want to do, and he was raising Cain about it, - then he said all of a sudden, 'Gladys, you can't do that—I'm Bubber's little boy.' He certainly believes in pulling every string imaginable. When I do something for him that he considers particularly nice, his face will brighten up so and break into smiles, and he'll say, 'Tanks, Gladys! Tanks!' putting all the expression in the world in it. The other day he asked me something and I answered him, or did something for him (I don't remember which), and he said, 'That's fine, Gladys! You're a nice girl.'"

Without siblings or a consistent circle of friends,

T.J.'s understanding of the concept of sharing took some time to develop. Writing about Roddey's visit to T.J. in August 1940, Gladys recounted an incident between the two boys. "He came to me and said 'Gladys, Roddey is a bad boy—he won't share his toys.' Mind you, he only had the rifle to share! I said that's what's the trouble with the world today; powerful countries wanting small, weak ones to 'share' what little they've got. Thos. Jeff. learned about sharing in one of his Sunday school lessons, so he began to apply it—but as applying to the other fellow, which is how we usually make application. Always when considering an ideal condition, we begin to think about what the other fellow ought to do, rather than beginning with ourselves."

Even Edgar noted T.J.'s lack of understanding about sharing. In an October 9, 1940, letter, Edgar wrote, "…the little fellow here has to have a birthday present every time he hears any one in the vicinity had a birthday party…."

T.J. recalled that when he was a very young child, the Cayce house felt like a real home, but the older he got and the more popular Mr. Cayce became, the more it felt like a hotel. That's because Cayce drew people like a magnet.

"They would come to him with desperate needs," T.J. said. "He would just go to sleep and tell them what to do. Instead of them leaving, they'd often stay for long periods of time. There were always six or seven people at any given time occupying the upstairs bedrooms. Some of them struck me as being strange—as if they were from a different planet. There were people from all over the world; both famous and lesser-known souls who came to ask him questions."

T.J. only got to know the people who worked there during the day putting together the A.R.E. "There was so much to do in those days," he reflected. "Those people came there to do something. They were on duty all the time. They were friendly and nice and had good vibes. I never thought of needing anything other than what they provided. It was a nice place to live. Nobody ever yelled at anybody."

Since souls tend to incarnate together, it's not surprising that everyone in the Cayce house had been together through many lifetimes. T.J. compared it to brokering a deal. "You come back and come back and come back and finally, hopefully, we all get something done and high-five it."

When he was about three years old, T.J. started understanding where he was and what was going on. He met some truly unbelievable people before and after Mr. Cayce was gone. "There were a great number of people who had been alive during the life of Christ and some biblical characters from much earlier," he recalled. "There was Mary Magdalene and several disciples, including Hugh Lynn, who had been Andrew."

The "who's who" of historical significance living at the Cayce household was not lost on anyone. A friend of the Cayces wrote: "Good gracious, with all of these pre-important people such as Thomas Jefferson – Alexander the Great [1208], Eli Whitney [2012], and [2005] and [2004]'s prospects around us, I feel about as important as a peanut! If my mother [2029] turns out to be Queen Elizabeth or Martha Washington, I'm going to stop speaking to her! I'm mad because I wasn't at least a *friend* of Columbus, or Napoleon's, or *somebody's*. But I guess being your friend now, is *much* more important!"

Even though he was a child and did not fully understand how these souls impacted history in their prior lifetimes, T.J. knew he was in the company of an extraordinary group of people.

"So there I am sharing this house with all these cool people; folks that you don't exactly meet at the poolroom," he said. "It was a group of heavy-duty souls. I wasn't aware of that until later, but for the most part, they were all nice to me. We were a family in the truest sense of the word. We had a house full of people talking about reincarnation, knowing who we each had been before. Everybody in that place was just wonderful. I was a fortunate kid to have grown up in that kind of a place, although I have to admit, I grew a little tired of getting patted on the head!"

Several of those head-patters stand out in his memory, including Mae St. Clair, Lydia Schrader Gray, and Thomas Sugrue.

T.J. described Mae as being full of energy, and when he was playing the aura game, he always chose her because her aura was the easiest to check out. T.J. said that

Mae's family lived in Oceana where they grew flowers. Mae and T.J.'s mother were friends and were a lot alike. If T.J. did something wrong, Mae would send him to the mimeograph machine.

Lydia Schrader Gray was what T.J. referred to as "the house monitor." He hid every time he saw her. Nonetheless, he acknowledged that she was an important part of the household.

"I did not dislike her, but she stared at me a lot and that scared me," he said. "She was like a schoolmarm who stood with her hands on her hips. If she had been in boot camp, she would have made a great drill sergeant. You just did not mess with her. She was definitely into Mr. Cayce's work, no question about that."

Another of his favorites was Thomas Sugrue, author of *There Is a River*. T.J. described Sugrue as a neat man who was really smart. "He was a person I would always run to and tell him what Mr. Cayce and I did that day. He wanted to know what went on during our sessions on the pier and I'd tell him he had to give me something for me to share that information, so he would bribe me with candy bars."

T.J. related an amusing story about Sugrue. Mr. Cayce had a parrot named Polly and T.J. trained her to say, "Hi Tom, Hi Tom, Get to Work!" The parrot lived on the porch and there were French doors at either end. Sugrue, who was in a wheelchair, liked to have T.J. push him around and through those doors, almost like a mouse on a treadmill.

"Sometimes we'd go so fast he'd almost gag from laughter," T.J. said. "One time when Polly started saying 'Hi Tom' he got so excited and laughed so much that he fell out of the chair and on to the floor. I didn't know what to do, but sure enough, it no sooner happened and out comes Mr. Cayce to help us. He brought iced tea and Coca-Cola with him and we sat there laughing after putting Tom back in the chair."

T.J. was six years old when *There Is a River* was published, but even at that young age, he knew enough to ask for his own autographed copy.

ORDER BLANK

Association for Research
and Enlightenment, Inc.
Virginia Beach, Va.

Attention: Mrs. Edgar Cayce

Please reserve for me... One ...copies of
THERE IS A RIVER, The Story of Edgar Cayce,
by Thomas Sugrue.

I understand that I will receive a numbered
copy, signed by Edgar Cayce, with a personal message for me.

Enclosed find. $5.00 . for. One ...
copies at five dollars ($5.00) each.

NAME Thomas Jefferson Davis

ADDRESS Arctic Crescent,

CITY Virginia Beach,

STATE Virginia.

In a letter to Boyd on August 28, 1942, Gladys wrote: "Thos. Jeff. kept asking 'Eddie Cayce' to let him empty his pig bank and buy the book, 'There is a River.' He insists he wants one for his very own—bless his heart. I tried to save up enough to reserve one for him, but I haven't been able to do it yet—$5 is a lot of money, extra, that is, when there is so much expense. Sept. 15th is the limit on the special edition, so maybe I can still get it before it is too late."

T.J. understood that Tom Sugrue was special—the kind of guy he liked to see around Mr. Cayce. That was because most of the people who ended up staying at the Cayce home had the same energy as Cayce and although a young child, T.J. understood that.

While many of the people who came were loving souls and he enjoyed their company, T.J. said there were a few exceptions. He recalled a time when a college professor and some of his students showed up.

"I was standing by the door minding my own business when what happened next was straight out of a movie," he said. "When they found out who I had been in a past life, they covered me with the American flag, threw me in the closet, and started chanting some really crazy stuff over me. I tried to get out of there, but they kept the door shut. There was a little light coming down from the stairs, but still it was dark and to a little kid, it was frightening. Another time some people wanted to hypnotize me and find out where Alexander the Great was buried because they wanted to find treasure."

From a very early age, T.J. knew how much Edgar loved him and looking at the photos of the two of them archived in the vault, there is no denying the close bond they shared. Even to the casual observer, those photos bring tears to the eyes. In a letter dated October 9, 1940, Edgar spoke of T.J. going off to kindergarten. "... saw him just start off with his raincoat of which he is very proud—believe me he is some boy."

Cayce's affection for T.J. was further stated in a letter to [#464] on January 2, 1941. "Had no children here this year for Christmas and missed it very much—How far is 4505 Behrwald Ave from you—a Mrs. S. Smith lives there I believe and that is where the young man we think so much of is visiting—with his Mother Mrs. Boyd Davis—the child is T.J. Davis, am sure have spoken of him to you—if not too much trouble with you would call them—just tell them or Mrs. Davis you are a friend of mine and am sure she will be glad to hear—and possibly she can come by would like for you to see that boy —he is about 4-½ now but we all about worship him here. He is a nephew of Miss Davis my Secy. She has been Secy. for 17 years and has lived in the house with us all these years—so must be very nice—or we very nice—to have gotten along with out any scraps."

Edgar knew that there would come a time when he wouldn't be around for T.J. Almost as if sensing he would not have as much time with the boy as he hoped, he took T.J. to the beach. As they were walking through the sand dunes, Edgar stopped to take a picture and told T.J.,

"We're going on a scavenger hunt today. Do you want to go on a scavenger hunt?"

"Sure," the boy replied eagerly.

"Well, you need something to remember me by just in case; something that's related to you." T.J. didn't know what that meant, but Edgar told him he'd find it on a pyramid.

T.J. said, "We continued to walk along the beach and I came across a ring sitting on a pyramid of sand, which was common on the beach. An old crab would die and the sand would form around its body. The ring was on the sand so I just reached down and took it. He said, 'There you go. You never know.' The ring didn't fit then but I soon grew into it and wear it to this day."

Chapter Twelve
The Enchanting Experiences of a Small Child

Edgar and T.J. on the pier with the willow tree. (ECF#1031)

While most children associate their education with the schools they attended, T.J.'s classroom was through the backdoor of the Cayce house and out on to the pier that jetted out on to the lake. Edgar and T.J. started fishing together when T.J. was old enough to hold a fishing pole. This was one of their favorite activities, and T.J. came to treasure the times they spent on the pier. When he could, Edgar took T.J. fishing nearly every day. T.J. said it was Edgar's way of relaxing and getting away from the pressure of doing so many readings.

During World War II, however, Cayce was engaged in critical work, so there were days when he was working and couldn't get away to fish. It was then that T.J. would play in the house or out in the yard. When he got older, he would go down to the beach on his own, but as a rule, most of their time together was spent on that pier.

During those times, T.J. didn't talk much—he just listened. Edgar would go on and on and T.J. would just keep asking questions, which his mentor always answered.

"It seemed so natural to me when he addressed me as if I were ten thousand years old, and if you listened in on our conversations, you would have thought the same thing. As a child, if you are spoken to as if you held all the wisdom of the ages in your soul, you don't know this is not the way other people communicate. Since I was somewhat isolated from the outside world and grew up very differently from other children, I had no idea of how to talk to, much less relate to, other kids my age. After Mr. Cayce died, that led to a lot of trouble for me, but as long as Mr. Cayce was alive and acting as my mentor, I was fine."

The pier outside their backdoor was a unique classroom where the elder mentor infused wisdom into his young charge. While Edgar could not control what formal schooling T.J.'s parents chose for their son, he used the pier to groom the young boy for the work that he had hoped he'd grow into.

"At first I did not know this, but I realize now that I was getting an incomparable education out on that pier," T.J. said. "We had hours of conversations in which he would tell me the things he felt were important for me to know. When I grew older, he began actual lessons where he taught me how to do some of the things he did. For instance, he explained all about dreams. I got so good at dreams, I could get in a dream and move around and ask questions. It wasn't as if I were dreaming at all. We talked about karma, grace, attitudes, emotions, and what was expected of us as souls since we were all related to God and to each other."

When T.J. was around five years old, Cayce began teaching him about thought forms and vibrations. T.J. said Edgar often used examples in nature to teach his lessons. At one point Edgar wanted to show T.J. the difference between a positive and negative thought form, so he used an example in horticulture. He gave the boy a handful of seeds and some dirt and told him to plant the seeds in two different pots. He instructed T.J. to yell at one of the pots, tell it that it was not going to be worth anything, and play horrible music around it. He told the boy to sing softly to the other plant, play beautiful music, say it was going to reach its fullest and highest potential, and take very good care of it. T.J. gave them both the same amount of plant food and water, but that was it.

When the plants came up, the one that he yelled at grew very little and then just fell over and died. The other plant that he cared for in a loving way—much the same way that he'd want to be cared for—grew by leaps and bounds.

"The lesson was that thoughts go places," T.J. reflected. "You have attitudes and your emotions affect everything. This experiment was an indication to me that everything that's alive has a consciousness and wants to be treated with love."

There wasn't much that irritated T.J. while they were out on that pier except for having to sit out in the hot sun—something he complained about all the time. Tired of hearing the boy whine about the heat, Edgar told T.J. that he'd fix that situation the next day and everything would be just fine. He took a small weeping willow tree out of the ground and replanted it in a box so it could float around the pier. He had a rope on it and if the sun got really hot, T.J. could pull on the rope and the little tree would come over to where they were and he'd be able to sit in the shade. "That's how cool a man he was," T.J. said as he smiled.

There was one stipulation to T.J.'s having that shade tree, however, and that was that he had to become friends with it. Just like the lesson Edgar taught the boy with the seedlings he planted, T.J. had to tell the tree it was beautiful and that it was going to grow to its fullest and highest potential.

"There we were, sitting in the shade of this tree, with Mr. Cayce telling this little kid what the deal was with humans," T.J. said. "How many children get that kind of an education from their parents?"

The Creation Story

Of all the lessons on the pier, the one about creation was—and still is—the most beautiful story T.J. ever heard.

"The creation story was my first official lesson," he said. "He started with creation so I would know who and what we are as human beings, where we came from, why we are here, and where we're going. He no doubt spent a great deal of time telling me that story because he felt it was crucial that I remember it so that I could share it later."

As with all of T.J.'s lessons, when Edgar told him the creation story, he did it in a way a young child could understand. The following is T.J.'s recollection of that lesson.

"On the first day of my lesson, we were coming on the pier and he stopped to pick up a dandelion—one of those little puffballs. Then he blew on it and all the little seeds floated off the stem. One minute they were together and the next they were apart, but they still came from the same source. He said, 'That's us. We are the seeds, the souls. We are part of the One and we are all connected, but we all went our separate ways. Not all the little seeds came to earth. Some went other places.' He added that those who came to earth knew the plan and understood what we were supposed to do. Before we left, the Creator said, 'If you go there and you get stuck in matter, then you have to learn how to take care of the place.'

"Mr. Cayce continued his story, describing us as light beings that came floating down to earth like those little dandelion seeds. When we first got here we were just a soul—like Casper the Friendly Ghost. I imagine we didn't have a body yet. Our form was much different than it is now. We communicated with each other through sound and dance—much the same way as the fairies I encountered later in Mr. Cayce's garden.

"So there we were, visiting this planet, acting as if we're on vacation on some tropical island. No cars or houses—just beautiful water, sky, wind, and animals. It was an unbelievable scene—no other souls had been here before. We were in awe of the earth and got caught up in its beauty. Somewhere along the line, we forgot the Creator's warning about staying too long. We spent our time sitting around in the trees and on the mountains looking around and enjoying what was going on in this material plane. We never dealt with matter before so we didn't take it very seriously. Early on, we could still leave. We didn't have to stay here. We could come and look and enjoy it and watch and see what was going on and then go back, but each time we came back we'd spend longer periods of time here, making it harder to leave.

"Eventually we became heavy like the material planet we inhabited. We started to find it more difficult to get out of here. We kept getting heavier until we couldn't leave anymore. It didn't take long before we knew we were stuck here and that was scary. We had stayed too long. We had not listened to the Creator, so we were on our own.

"We realized we had to make the best of a bad situation, so we started looking around for a body. As souls, we could do many mystical, magical things. In order to find bodies for ourselves, we began pushing our etheric bodies into things like trees and animals until we ended up looking like mythological characters—half human, half horse. What we needed was a body that could function here and do the will of God, but instead we had tree limbs for arms. We really screwed it up. We were ugly. There was chaos on the planet and no plan. We had totally messed up and everyone was freaking out.

"So God sent in another group of souls to come down and straighten us out. My aunt Gladys was one of those souls who came in to rescue those who were trapped here. She worked in the Temple Beautiful—a sort of metaphysical hospital—where they were trying to fix creatures that had pushed themselves into matter in some fashion. The rescue group knew that if we're going to be from this planet, we had to have a body that came literally from the same elements that made up the planet. Those who worked in the Temple Beautiful took apart the distorted bodies and gave them new bodies—the body that Amelius—who was Adam—had. And that's when the Garden of Eden story began.

"There was a third group of souls who came in and Christ was among this last group. He had a few earlier lifetimes, too. He just didn't come and get crucified. He was here at the beginning—Adam as a matter of fact. So we finally had someone on board who was clear thinking and realized that God has a plan. We were part of that plan and we needed to pay attention to what was going on.

"Mr. Cayce told me that our purpose for being here is to be a companion with God whom he referred to as the Creative Force. Obviously there is a lot of room for improvement. The reason we got sidetracked has to do with free will, which Mr. Cayce said we were given as a gift from God. We were allowed to go wherever we wanted. But giving us free will was like giving us a credit card with unlimited spending. We started being abusive right off the bat. Our selfish desire to stay here for aggrandizement was overpowering so before the human race was even created, we were in a jam. That's pretty much where our problems began. Every selfish desire that came out of us at that point is still with us today. It especially shows up in religion and politics. We can be a nasty group of people if we want to be. That's the destructive force within us that we turn loose, but the destructive force was never what we were supposed to be. We have a lot of karma to work out and now is a good time to stand up and say this can't go on anymore."

T.J. said he found the creation story an interesting topic because most children don't know where we came from.

"They think of Adam and Eve and some dirt, putting a couple of people together, an apple and a snake and that's it, but it's not like that at all. Many people believe we came from the Big Bang or are descended from apes. You seldom, if ever, read the creation story as Mr. Cayce told it. It is so laughable to me that someone would deny Mr. Cayce's rendition of how life emerged on earth because they think his version is impossible. They would rather believe we evolved from apes or that someone threw a hand grenade out there and created the universe. None of these folks talk about a divine plan. Mr. Cayce did and gave us a step-by-step lesson in why we're here. It is extraordinary and at the same time overwhelming. The value of knowing the creation story is that it helps us find out who we are, why we're here, and where we're going. That's big-time stuff."

The Aura Game

T.J. said Edgar enjoyed playing games and early on he decided that in order to hold the young boy's attention, everything had to be made into a game. When he decided it was time for T.J. to learn to see colors around everything, he devised what he called the aura game.

The game began one afternoon when Edgar asked T.J. if he could see auras. "I'm sure I said no because I didn't know what an aura was," T.J. said. Cayce explained to the boy that an aura was like a picture—it was an energy field that surrounds everything that's alive and you can see it. He said he would show T.J. how to do it.

"He told me that everything that is alive has a vibration and a color that comes with it, but the colors are not always the same," T.J. said. "They fluctuate according to how healthy and happy we are. He explained that's how he saw people when they were sick. If they had a damaged this or a damaged that, the color around that area was muddy so he knew right away where to start looking for some of their troubles."

Edgar told T.J. that it was really valuable to know how to see auras because it would save him from getting into trouble. For instance, if he saw someone in the parking lot and they were surrounded by a murky color, he needed to get away from them. So being able to see auras was a real big deal for T.J., who practiced it with all his might, but couldn't quite get the knack of it. Then one day they were on the pier and a storm came up. Edgar asked T.J. if he could see the colors on the trees, to which T.J. responded no, that everything looked green to him. Edgar encouraged him to try again by looking around the edges of the trees. The boy saw nothing and the storm came and left.

Edgar did not give up and continued on and on with this lesson. Then after a few months of T.J. trying to see auras, the two were going out to fish again. T.J. ran out early to get on the pier so he could get the seat on the left because Edgar used to clean the fish on the right and T.J. didn't want to see or smell that. As he ran out to the pier, he passed a little tree that was blinking like a Christmas tree, with little lights that seemed to be vibrating.

"It scared me and I ran back inside, yelling, 'The tree's on fire!' Mr. Cayce came out and said—'Oh no, that's the aura. You've seen an aura!' I didn't know what to think. I stared at that tree for days."

Another time when they were on the pier, T.J. got so excited when he saw an aura that he nearly fell into the water. Edgar reached down and grabbed the boy.

"What's going on?" he asked and then realized what had happen. "Oh, you see a color?"

"Yes, I do," T.J. responded eagerly. "I saw orange on this tree across the lake. It was not on the leaves—they were green—but outside was orange and then outside the orange was dark brown, kind of muddy brown."

"Yes, that tree is damaged and it's going to die," Edgar explained.

T.J. said they had just transplanted that tree so part of it was dying. He told Edgar that part of the colors were fading and not looking too good. Edgar responded by saying that's what happens with auras. If you look at them, it's helpful. You can tell if someone is sick and where and then you can try to help. T.J. was proud of himself when he finally could see the aura in the trees. The whole process was amazing to him.

After that, T.J. got better and better at seeing auras. Once he became fairly proficient, Mr. Cayce raised the stakes.

"Okay, here's the deal in the aura game," Edgar told the boy. "You get to pick the person or whatever it is you want to concentrate on. If you get the colors at least fifty-percent right, we'll go fishing. But if you don't get it right, you're going to have to work in the garden."

T.J. hated working in the garden when it was hot, so he practiced very hard at seeing auras. Being a fairly smart child, he picked people in the house whose auras were explosive, like Mae St. Clair and Lydia Schrader Gray. He said their colors were like dynamite; flying all over the place. "I'd just say, 'Okay, this is what I see on Lydia.' Finally he got tired of my taking the easy way out and made me look at other people!"

Life Saver

T.J. could never fool Mr. Cayce the way other kids could lie and hide things from their parents. Edgar always knew where he was because he could read the boy's mind. He didn't just have vague ideas about what T.J. was thinking such as, "Well, T.J. is thinking about birds today." According to T.J., Edgar could repeat everything—word for word—of what was on his mind. If he was thinking—"Boy, it's really a rotten day," Edgar would say—"You were thinking, boy, it's really a rotten day"—not, "oh, you were thinking something about the day." There were times T.J. tried to trick him and when he was out of sight, he'd be thinking—"I'm climbing a tree"—but Edgar knew differently.

"To say that was a little uncomfortable is an understatement," T.J. said. "I really had to be on my best behavior and control my thoughts, which is not an easy thing for a child to do."

T.J. recalled that Edgar especially liked to play

cards. When it would rain the two of them would play Fish. Edgar would deal out five or six cards and T.J. would pick them up and look at them, having no idea what these cards were.

Edgar explained the game to the boy. "I ask you if you have these cards and if you don't, you have to draw a card out of the pack. So, let's go. Give me all your eights."

T.J. said he looked at Edgar with no expression on his face. "I didn't know an eight from a three or a queen from a hippopotamus," he said. "So I'd have my cards in my hands facing me and without looking at them, he pointed to each and said, 'This is an eight. This is a four. This is a six.' Or he'd say, 'Give me all your queens. It's this one right here and this one over there.' He was looking through the cards and that really scared me, so I knew early on that I could never lie to him. Imagine being a kid and not being able to lie? When he died, I lied constantly. I just could not help myself. I got such a thrill out of lying and being able to get away with it!"

Having the ability to know what T.J. was thinking meant he always knew where the boy was and that saved T.J.'s life several times. T.J. was not supposed to go out on the pier by himself. He always had to be with somebody, but he wasn't easy to care for because he was always sneaking away. When Cayce was giving a reading, everyone was with him who normally would be watching T.J., so even though the boy was expected to remain in the house, on occasion he would sneak out.

"One time he was inside giving a reading and I got

away from Georgiana, who was supposed to be watching me," T.J. recalled. "I wandered down to the lake and became mesmerized by a turtle swimming off the side of the pier. Because I was still so young, the depth of the water there was well over my head. I didn't know how to swim, so had I fallen in, I surely would have drowned. As I bent over to get a closer look at the turtle, Mr. Cayce— while still in a trance state—stopped and said something like, 'Gladys, you better get T, he's going to fall in the lake and probably drown.' There is no way anyone could have seen me from that room because the window was high and everyone, being seated around Mr. Cayce, did not have a view of the lake. Gladys stopped taking dictation, got up and looked out the window. There I was teetering back and forth on the pier, trying to get the turtle out of the water. Gladys ran out, grabbed me by the seat of the pants, and brought me back inside. What is so remarkable about this was that Mr. Cayce was doing several things at once—all while in a trance. If he hadn't been who he was, I would have been at the bottom of the lake."

This was not the only time that Cayce saved T.J. from drowning. Once it happened while they were on the pier fishing.

"We had been talking about meditation, which I diligently had been practicing all week," T.J. said. "I was getting to the point where I thought I might actually be meditating, but in reality what I was doing was falling asleep. So we're fishing, and since I'm not catching any fish, I decided I would try to meditate while we're sitting there. I had my fishing pole in the water and I got a bite but the force of the bite started to drag me off the pier.

Mr. Cayce just reached over and grabbed me by the collar and said, 'Okay, that's twice. You have to be cool by the lake because you're not good with water.' This had to be a reference to a past life, but he never explained what he meant by that."

Fairies and Elementals

T.J. couldn't remember a time when he wasn't doing something in the garden. He had a real love-hate relationship with that plot of land. He hated it because it was so hot to be out there in the summer, but he loved it because sometimes it could be fun. Cayce had a large asparagus garden that was about as tall as T.J., so to a child it was like playing in a little shaded forest.

One day Edgar told the boy that he'd meet him in the garden in a few minutes and that T.J. should go ahead, work on the asparagus, and look at the colors until Cayce arrived. T.J. went to the garden and did his chores, getting on his hands and knees, moving the dirt around and making sure the plants could breathe.

"So I'm out there tilling around each asparagus plant and I heard this little buzzing noise," T.J said. "Suddenly this thing flew out at me and touched me right on the forehead. At first I thought it was a bee or a hummingbird until I looked closer. It had a face, but its body was like a weed or an herb. It was an honest-to-goodness fairy, and they were all over the garden. They scared me so much that I wouldn't be surprised if I wet my pants. I came running out of the garden so fast that my feet were flying in front of me almost at a forty-five-degree angle as I scampered to get out of there. I had no idea what they were, but I knew that you didn't see little people flying around outside in the weeds.

"Mr. Cayce came out about this time and asked what colors I saw. I answered, 'Colors? There are little bird people in there buzzing around!'

"'No, no, no,' he said, comforting me. 'Those are fairies—elementals—and they take care of the garden. They're in charge of all the earth, everything that grows, that's their job. They're friendly if you're friendly. Go back and play with them. Check out their colors.'"

After T.J. got over the initial shock of actually seeing them and realizing it wasn't all in his head, that's exactly what he did. He got brave and looked at them a little closer. Edgar told him that to see them clearly he should just keep staring at the space between them.

"They looked like people, but they also looked like hummingbirds," T.J. said. "They were green and dark brown and had a pointed nose, but no ears, and had legs that looked like sticks. They didn't wear clothing or shoes. You could nearly see through them and they appeared to have wings. I would go out in the morning, and they were busy flying around. They were in charge of making sure there was peace and harmony there, not so much from me, but from the mice that wanted to come in there and attack the plants. If I could see one that was really happy, I tried to make friends. Eventually they were able to communicate with me and I with them. They didn't actually talk. They would buzz at me and in my mind—'mind's the builder'—I could hear what they were saying. They weren't using words. They were conveying thoughts, like 'it's nice out today.' They would sometimes come in my room at night and buzz around."

T.J. learned they communicated through music and color. In his mind he knew what they were up to and also by different sounds and body language he could tell what was going on. It would just be in his head, and then he would think something and they would smile.

"They would make a noise, like a beautiful sound that I almost could understand," he said. "Their music reminded me of music of the spheres, and I liked it right away. The sound came with a color that popped in my head. I didn't talk back because I wasn't good at singing and I didn't know enough about color. I do remember if I made the right sound, they sometimes could understand what I was saying, but I was not very good at it and frankly, I didn't think they cared what I said. Most of the time they probably were just telling me to move along because they had work to do."

Even at that age T.J. said he felt a little stupid talking to fairies, but they were the first creatures around which he could see auras. Even though their auras looked pleasant, he still could never get used to them flying around in the yard. It made him uncomfortable but because Edgar seemed at ease with them, eventually it got to be okay with the boy.

T.J. said it was very crowded in the garden because the fairies weren't the only ones there. Other creatures occupied that space as well, including what he described as ugly frog-looking things. He said he never got in good with them and they would chase him relentlessly, but he thought the fairies were cool and soon had the distinction of being the only kid at Virginia Beach who had fairies for friends.

T.J. continued to see elementals in one form or another for many years after that. When he was in his late teens and still living at home, he described an incident in his bedroom one evening that he considers as one of the most astounding things that he ever experienced.

"I should say up front that I didn't drink alcohol, and I hadn't ingested anything that would have caused me to see this!" he prefaced. "I was stone cold sober and totally aware of my surroundings. The windows were shut, and I was sitting there listening to music when suddenly a blue sphere floated right through the wall. Now normally a person would look at that and scream, but it didn't freak me out a bit because having lived with Edgar Cayce, absolutely nothing surprised me. My first inclination was to try and communicate with the sphere. It had little pyramid-shaped lights all connected together and was hollow in the middle. It was spinning as it came into the room. I looked at it and said, 'What is this? Am I under surveillance or what? Okay, give me a sign. What are you?'"

Over in the corner he had a jar with peacock feathers in it. The sphere whipped over there and blew the feathers all over the room. With that, T.J. left his room to find Gladys and ask her to come and look at it.

"Oh, it's an elemental," she said matter-of-factly.

"That's not an elemental," T.J. protested. "I know elementals. This thing is coming through the wall."

Gladys didn't pay attention to what T.J. was saying and went back to cooking dinner. He said she didn't talk about it again, almost as if she found it boring. But to T.J. it was a big deal, especially since it had chosen to come into his room. It left right away and even though he always thought it would come back, it never did.

This isn't to say the experience did not have a significant impact on T.J. That night he had a very vivid dream about his former mentor that he believes was a past-life memory.

"Mr. Cayce came to the house. He got me and said we were going on a trip. He had a crystal piece and it was slender and had a little ball at the end of it. It was all one piece and we got on this thing—straddled it like a horse—and it took off. It was like Harry Potter. We went flying to Egypt and we went underground and we were going on this long, speedy trip through these passageways and on either side were these hieroglyphics. They were beautiful. I couldn't read them but they were different colors. We went into this huge circular place with high ceilings, and in the middle was a pyramid inside the pyramid, but they were clear. Inside each block of pyramid was a person just sitting in it. We got off, walked around, and he said: 'This is for you. You get in here.' So he opened the thing up and I sat in there and the whole pyramid took off. It went right up through the main pyramid. It was the same dimensions almost, only smaller and clear. We went right through the pyramid and traveled, just zoned around a little bit, and it settled down right in front of the Sphinx. We got out. He was in the little box. There was a bunch of people—we all got out of this little box. Mr. Cayce opened the door and we went down into this staircase and that's where the Hall of Records was and he showed them to me. He said: 'Don't forget. This is real stuff.'"

Stefanella

As a very young child, T.J. understood that he lived in a place that was really special. But he also was cognizant that there was no one there his size. He did not think in terms of age. He thought only in terms of size. He complained about that often, believing he always would be small.

Edgar realized T.J. needed a friend. Just as he did when T.J. complained for the umpteenth time about how hot it was on the pier, Edgar addressed the issue of finding a friend by telling the boy, "We'll work on that. Don't worry about it. I'll try to dig up a play mate for you."

The next day Edgar and T.J. were fishing when T.J. heard footsteps running on the pier, followed by violin music. T.J. turned around and saw a pretty little girl about his size playing the violin.

Edgar said, "This will be your friend for a while. Her name is Stefanella."

All T.J. remembers saying is, "Oh cool!"

So now T.J. had a friend his age. At first he thought Stefie was a real person; that perhaps she was a neighbor's child. As a five-year-old, T.J. was impressionable and it was easy for him to believe someone would come out on the pier playing a violin and wanting to hang out with him. He shared Stefie's love of music so he tried to play as well but he wasn't very good at it. Stefie would continue to play the violin and sing in Italian. T.J. recalled when she would get lost in her music, she would lose her physical presence and fade in and out. At those times he didn't want to touch her because it looked as if he could go right through her.

Stefie never came into the house, but whenever T.J. was outside she always seemed to be there and he got to play with her for long periods of time. It didn't occur to him until weeks later that she was not a real person.

"I often wondered how Mr. Cayce did it," he mused. "Did he hang out a notice somewhere in the Universe that said: HELP WANTED—SOMEONE TO HANG OUT WITH T.J. BECAUSE HE HAS NO FRIENDS?"

Whether she was living or in spirit, having Stefie there made things easier for T.J. They played together all the time, often including the fairies in their playtime. T.J. never understood anything Stefie said because she only spoke in Italian so they communicated telepathically. T.J. admitted he was a little afraid of her at first but after awhile it didn't seem to matter. She remained his companion until Cayce died and T.J. never saw her again—at least not in the way he had as a child, as we will see in chapter 15: "Retracing the Past."

An Evening of Laughter and Levitation

T.J. said Cayce had many visitors from India. When they came to the house, the Cayces prepared a substantial meal of fish and rice, which T.J. liked. After dinner everyone took a walk by the lake.

One particular visit stood out in T.J.'s memory. "I should have realized it would be a special night because that day I caught twelve fish. I usually caught one or two fish a month, but that day I caught twelve. Conveniently, that night we were having twelve people for dinner, so we were able to eat all the fish I caught and that made me feel special. Mr. Cayce, who usually always caught more fish than I did, caught just two that day and gave those to Captain Billy, a very stoic-looking heron who usually came along when we went fishing. He'd stand there on his long stick legs and watch us. Mr. Cayce would always throw Captain Billy a fish or two."

T.J. described their Indian guests as a man, his sister who wore a lot of scarves, and her son, who T.J. guessed was in his early twenties. The Cayces had a long dinner table and everybody living in the house at that time was there. T.J. said he didn't pay too much attention to their guests because he hardly understood anything they said, even though they spoke fairly good English.

After dinner, T.J. helped Mrs. Cayce with the dishes. When everyone went outside to take a walk by the lake, she let him join them as well. Earlier T.J. and Edgar had been talking about the pyramids.

"As Ra Ta, he had been one of the persons responsible for building the pyramids," T.J. said. "I had been bugging him about that, telling him I didn't believe that slaves built the pyramids, that I thought something else happened. After all, you couldn't pick up those giant stones. He said no, it was the same principle that makes iron float."

During the walk, T.J. said Edgar took him aside and reminded him about their talk about levitation and how it's the same principle as the way iron floats in water. He told T.J. he would show him how they built the pyramid. His Indian guests said it would be all right if T.J. watched from the top of the stairs. So Cayce told T.J. if he wanted to see how iron floats in water, to be at the top of the stairs when they went into the living room.

T.J. was excited about that because he knew iron couldn't float in water. He thought Edgar was just saying that to trick him. At the same time, his imagination was working overtime. He knew if he was being invited to watch from the top of the stairs, that meant something extraordinary was going to happen and the fact that Mr. Cayce specifically invited him to watch this time made him feel "really cool."

"I knew he only did that when he felt I could handle whatever I was going to see," T.J. said. "Plus I felt comfortable there because I had easy access to the tiny bathroom under the staircase. If I got scared, I ran down there to hide."

The only problem was that it was getting late. T.J. fought to stay awake, but it was hard. He knew sometimes these visits in the living room would go on and on into the night. He decided he wanted to catch some sleep, so he left, but then Gladys came up and said, "T, you have to watch this because it's going to be good." He said okay and went to his designated spot.

T.J. recalls there were six people in the living room—Mr. and Mrs. Cayce, Gladys, and the three visitors.

"They were just sitting and talking and then they all got up and the young man reclined on the floor next to the couch. They all took positions around him. Then they all started humming, especially the Indian gentleman. I kept waiting for words to be sung, but it was just humming. It was similar to the 'ohm' sound in meditation, but not quite that. The sound was very peculiar, and it kept evolving into a chant of some sort until it almost hurt my ears. This went on for about ten minutes. I was interested and a little nervous at the same time. When the sound reached a crescendo, they lifted the young man right off the floor without touching him, as if he was on strings. He rose about a foot and a half and he stayed there the longest time. The sound they were making slowly diminished, like a light dimming, and then he was lowered back down on the couch and went to sleep. The vibrations in the room were so strong. I'm surprised they didn't put lead in my pants so I wouldn't float upwards."

The next day T.J. asked Mr. Cayce what that was all about and how it was that he was just floating in the air.

"He said, 'Remember all our talks on the pyramids? Remember how that happened? They didn't have twenty-five million people with ropes dragging these stones up across the Sinai to lay them down. They would levitate them. Remember in Atlantis people levitated stuff—it was just a matter of doing it. I can't explain it to you right now, but it works and now you've seen it and we've talked about it.'"

T.J. said when he saw this happen, he thought it was cool. "Most people would have run out the door and called 911 (if we had had 911 back then!). So many weird things that happened in that house that this guy floating around in the air wasn't all that spectacular, but it didn't matter because I had no one I could talk to about this. My first thought was wondering whether I could do that. I tried often after that, but I couldn't pick up anything. To this day I can see it, but I still question—did that really happen? Then I realize—yes, it really did. I saw things later that were more bizarre than this, but that levitation was big and always stuck in my memory."

Talking to Ghosts

T.J. said spirits came to visit quite often. He remembers Edgar commenting that someone was around that more than likely walked through the wall rather than the door. During Edgar's weekly talks, for instance, the room would be filled with people and every seat taken. The evening usually began by Lydia Schrader Gray introducing Cayce to the group. T.J. said that on more than one occasion, Cayce held her up from making the introduction because he was waiting for certain souls to join the group.

"He knew every one of them and he'd actually wait for them to be seated," T.J. laughed. "They were almost fairy-like and did not resemble real people. Even as a child, I could see the energy forming shapes. I couldn't see them dressed in suits or wearing watches, but I could tell something nonphysical had come into the room. It was kind of spooky. They'd just walk in the room and then he'd begin. As things settled down, they'd disappear."

Michael the Archangel

T.J. often wondered what went on in the Cayce living room when so many adults were gathered. Out of curiosity, he'd often quietly tiptoe to the landing at the top of the stairs to get a peek at what was happening downstairs. He remembers one such clandestine viewing in particular when he was seven. Edgar and Gertrude Cayce, June and Harmon Bro, Gladys, and a few others were gathered together. The reading started quietly enough, but suddenly T.J. said a huge noise came out of Mr. Cayce's mouth—"*Bow thine heads, ye children of men! For I, Michael, Lord of the Way, would speak with thee! Ye generation of vipers, ye adulterous generation, be warned*!" (294-208, T16).

"Everything in the house shook," T.J. recalled. "It was so unbelievable. I never heard anyone talk through Mr. Cayce before. I always thought he was pretty much in charge, but not this time. His voice was thundering and in a manner unlike Mr. Cayce in his waking state, began telling people off right and left."

T.J. said that incident scared him so much that he never spied on the adults again.

Fire at the Star of the Sea

[Author's Note: I am including this story because it is one that T.J. told repeatedly to numerous audiences. In doing research on the fire at the Star of the Sea Catholic Church, however, I found many discrepancies in the dates, putting into question the accuracy of T.J.'s version. However, since it is a story he clearly loved to tell, I am including it here, along with the research I did to try and recreate an accurate timeline. I leave it to you to just sit back and enjoy the story, remembering what I said earlier about the accuracy of memory recall.]

Like most young boys, T.J. often got into hot water. When he was older and his horizons expanded, he found several playmates in the neighborhood. One of them was Joe, a boy about T.J.'s age who lived nearby with his father, who was the police chief, his mother, and two brothers. With only a small patch of woods separating their homes, Joe and T.J. played together often, hanging out or walking on the beach.

Joe had a BB gun and at first he only used it to shoot at trees and out over the lake. Then one day T.J. was getting ready to go down to his house when Joe yelled at him from the roof of the Star of the Sea, the Catholic church that was across the street.

"T.J., watch this," Joe yelled and then started shooting at him. T.J. was far enough away that by the time the shots got to him, they just bounced off. Still, he didn't like it and told him to stop, but Joe refused so T.J. got mad and for about a week the two friends didn't talk to each other. T.J. said during this period, it got to be so that if he walked by Joe's house and he was out, Joe would shoot at him.

"I didn't have a clue why he was doing this, but I knew I had to find a way to defend myself," said T.J. He remembered that Mr. Cayce had a yellow rain jacket. When T.J. put it on it went all the way down to his ankles and he had to roll up the sleeves. He thought of it as a yellow tank. He decided to wear it whenever he would walk by Joe's house so if he shot at T.J., it wouldn't hurt.

When even this did not deter Joe from his continual harassment with that BB gun, T.J. knew he had to find a way to stop him once and for all. In true Alexander fashion, he devised a plan of attack. This is his rendition of that event. Keep in mind this story was told from the perspective of nearly seventy years later.

"One day I saw him hiding in the churchyard behind the statue of Mary and baby Jesus," T.J. said. "When he realized I saw him, he decided he needed a better vantage point, so he climbed up to the top of the eaves and started to shoot at me again. But this time I was ready. I had received a toy bow and arrow set for Christmas. It wasn't anything that would cause lethal damage, but it did have a very strong bow. I thought about the bounty of cattails growing on the shore of the lake, so I went down there and pulled out five or six of them. I tied them to the arrow and then dipped the fuzzy part in the kerosene can that was in the back of the house. I had some matches on me, so I snuck up on Joe, lit the cattails, and fired the arrow in his general direction. The back of the arrow with the kerosene-dipped cattails was ablaze and I was astounded at how high and fast it flew. I actually was impressed with my newfound skill until the still-flaming arrow landed in a gutter filled with dry leaves, which quickly caught on fire and began to spread. Joe began yelling at me as he tried to put the fire out, but all he managed to do was spread the burning leaves and the fire got worse."

The boys both knew they were in big trouble. Joe scampered down and suddenly the two enemies were allies. They got on their bikes and rode a few blocks to the fire department. The guys at the firehouse knew the boys and vice versa, because the fire chief's kids were their playmates.

T.J. recalled how he and Joe were deflecting blame on each other. "So there is Joe yelling, 'T.J. set the church on fire!' Meanwhile, I'm declaring my innocence, saying that it was Joe's knocking around the leaves that did it. We were arguing back and forth, both of us worried about being blamed for this."

The fire crew drove to the church and put out the fire, but by then it had burned off about a quarter of the roof.

"Mr. Cayce and Gladys came out and stood next to me as we watched the firefighters putting out the flames," T.J. said. "Gladys was freaking out. I remember mimicking Mr. Cayce by telling her that everything was going to be just fine. I know that Mr. Cayce said something to me about it, but I don't remember what he said or whether any punishment came down because of it. I assumed he just knew I was trying to keep from getting shot by the BB gun."

This wasn't the first time T.J. had been caught playing with matches. One time he was in the living room and lit some matches. He heard Gladys coming into the room, so he put the matches under the sofa seat cushion. A short time later, smoke began to ascend from the sofa. Edgar pulled the sofa over to the fireplace and extinguished the smoldering seats before any damage was done to the rest of the house. The incident at the church, however, was far more serious and T.J. said he never played with matches after that.

Despite the damage he and Joe caused at the church, T.J. said that about a month after the fire, Father Brennan, the Irish parish priest, came over to talk to them about the fire.

"I liked him because of his Irish accent," T.J. said. "He liked Mr. Cayce, which I thought was unusual, but then I thought—well, they see fairies in Ireland. I see fairies and so did Mr. Cayce, so I thought we all fit together. He said he wanted to thank me because as a result of my good marksmanship and the fire, they were able to build an extension on to the church. Apparently the diocese had been contemplating moving the church elsewhere because it lacked a school. Father Brennan told this to the congregation and people began to chip in more, excited to fix up the place. As it turned out, the insurance claim from the fire and the donations from the congregation were enough not only to repair the church but also to build the classrooms that Father Brennan had wanted for so long. The disaster turned into a miracle."

In my attempt to corroborate T.J.'s story, I did some research into the history of the Star of the Sea, which was the first Catholic parish in Virginia Beach. On August 31, 2015, the *Catholic Virginian* published an article written by Eric Johnson, whose family rented the Cayce house from the A.R.E. during the 1960s. Entitled "Star of the Sea Celebrates 100th Birthday," it gave a rather different version of the famous fire and the subsequent building of the school.

Johnson, who was a student at the Star of the Sea, knew a great deal about the parish. In his article, he wrote that Father Brennan's tenure as pastor ended in 1950 and it was then that Father Nicholas Habets assumed that role. The article states, "It was during the tenure of Father Habets that Star of the Sea School was established." This would put it well after Edgar had died.

The article also disputes the date and location of the fire, stating:

"Early in the 1960s a fire destroyed the organ in the choir loft above the front door, completely burned the confessional in the back of the church, and blackened the original marble altar."

In T.J.'s defense, it very well could have been Father Brennan's dream to build a school and since acquiring funds and construction contracts and such takes a while, perhaps it took over five years before it actually happened and by then Father Brennan was gone. However, there is no mention of a fire in the 1940s that destroyed the roof and if, indeed, the fire took place in the early 1960s, Edgar would not have been alive to witness it . . . unless, of course, he was there in spirit standing next to T.J. Perhaps that's why no punishment was handed down!!

There is an interesting connection between the Star of the Sea and A.R.E. In the late 1970s, the school was in need of a playground. By then, the parish had owned the former Cayce property for years. The house still stood on the property. The article states: "To avoid having to pay for demolition of the house, parish leaders offered the house first to the Edgar Cayce Society to be moved to their properties on 67th Street. When they refused the gift, it was offered to the Virginia Beach Fire Department for practice in fighting fires."

In September 1976, a large crowd, including T.J., Gladys, and Eric Johnson and his family, gathered to watch the firefighters burn the house to the ground, and the land for the playground was cleared. T.J. said it was one of the saddest moments in his life to watch that house, where he shared so many loving moments with Edgar Cayce, destroyed by fire. Next to Cayce's death, T.J. remembered this as the most emotion-filled moment he shared with Gladys.

"That house had meant so much to both of us," he explained. "Gladys and I held hands as flames engulfed the house. At one point she whispered to me: 'It is just like in the garden.' I didn't know what she meant, but whatever it was, I knew she was referring to a similar scene we had both witnessed in a distant lifetime. For that reason, her words gave me comfort on a day that flooded us with both sad and happy memories of an earlier time when our soul family was all together."

Dealing with the Public's Perception

Even though T.J.'s friends and their parents knew of Edgar Cayce and what he did, T.J. understood at an early age that he had to be very careful about what he said to even his closest friends.

He remembered some happy times with his classmates when he was a little older. Gladys would drive T.J. and his schoolmates, including Joe Dunn and Bruce Murphy, around town. Sometimes she would take them to the drive-in movies. She would take a lawn chair and sit beside the car door while the boys watched the movies.

"We thought we were so cool," T.J. recalled. "Virginia Beach was a small town back then, and we all went to school with each other. I would go over to their houses, but I could tell there was a difference in their home environment and mine. Their parents were fine to me, but I could always sense an undercurrent."

Many of T.J.'s friends were not allowed to come to the Cayce house. If he went out with them after school, when it was time for him to go home, their parents would drop him off a block and a half from home.

"They would claim they didn't want to go down Pacific Avenue, but I knew the real reason was because they were scared to go up to the place," he said. "I understood why. Mr. Cayce was very different from them. The sign outside said, 'Association for Research and Enlightenment' and that was scary to some people driving down the street. First they thought Mr. Cayce was crazy. Then they thought I was crazy. But I never thought anything about it. As soon as I left their environment—be it their home or their car—it was almost as if someone were taking a photograph—click—and now I am back in the third or fourth dimension going back to seeing auras."

Straddling the "normal" and the "paranormal" world at the same time is difficult; at least it was for T.J. He felt as though he had one foot in one dimension and the other in another dimension. At first he thought it was okay to talk about what he knew, but he quickly learned not to share his experiences with anybody.

"The moment you tell somebody you can see color around things, they think you're nuts," he surmised. "It took me a long time to learn to keep my mouth shut. I didn't talk about this to any other human being in the world until I began sharing my experiences with A.R.E. members in the Charlottesville area."

T.J. said it was discouraging when he grew older to find that everyone didn't have the wonderful childhood that he had. After all, he lived with a man who could answer any question. Why are we here? What's the point? What are humans? Are we aliens? Where did we come from? What about all the animals? What about the trees? What's the deal here?

He often wondered why Edgar told him all of that. "He could have farmed me out or got a nanny to take care of me," he reflected.

During the '60s and '70s, T.J. spent a lot of time sitting on the great porch that surrounded the old A.R.E. hospital building. As he sat there thinking about everything, all the material Edgar shared boggled his mind and he said he could "actually feel" the vibration of the readings in the building behind him, as if they had a power of their own.

He first noticed this on a day when four young people showed up wearing backpacks and carrying water bottles. They climbed the steps and opened the door. T.J. was often the first person people would see when they'd come to the A.R.E. so he'd always warmly greet visitors, asking what brought them there. Most told him they came because they were interested in what they had heard about Mr. Cayce. One summer he estimated there were close to one hundred kids from all over the world who came to the A.R.E. and he had the opportunity to meet them all.

"I often get really sad reminiscing about those years because I miss all the people I knew at the A.R.E. in those early days. Now I'm just about the only one left. Mr. Cayce was such an incredible person. He saved my life all the time. Made sure I was comfortable. Taught me how to see colors. Told me that I had lived many times and this is why I was here this time. All of these conversations were meant to give me the tools I'd need to somehow be in a position to help out this country and the world."

T.J. said he was a lot like Edgar in that the things he believed in were so far out of the mainstream that it was hard for him to relate to anything or anyone. He wasn't a particularly good student and spent a lot of time staring out the window thinking about what it was going to be like in 2050 and where he would go when he died. Would he be able to hook up with his A.R.E. family again? Those were the kind of thoughts that occupied his mind as a child.

"When we sat on the pier together, I was just in

awe of Mr. Cayce," he reminisced. "Even though I was young, I knew I was sitting next to one of the greatest people in the world, yet he was fun to be with. Sometimes when he spoke, it almost seemed like I could put my hand through him. He would get so gossamer and caught up in what he was saying. It was just like his work. He was out there. He was going somewhere in his mind when we talked about things like karma and grace. You could ask him any question—and I must have asked him a million questions—and he would give you an answer. What an extraordinary opportunity that was."

After Edgar died, T.J. said he spent hours outside, lying on his back, looking up at the sky, wondering why he couldn't be like everyone else. There were times he wished he didn't know or hadn't seen any of the things he witnessed while with Mr. Cayce just because he felt so different from everyone else.

"I still feel that way and I'm still thought of as quite nuts by a lot of people because of all that I experienced and know to be true," he admitted. "Still, I consider myself as having one of the best educations a person can get in this time period. It's been frustrating for me because I feel as though I haven't been able to change what I wanted to change. I feel I really have let down a lot of souls that were depending on me to do something that I haven't been able to do yet. But I might live to be one hundred forty, and if I do, I'm more than halfway there."

Chapter Thirteen

Living with Gladys, His Guardian Angel

Gladys and T.J. in front of Star of the Sea on the pier.
(ECF#0978

T.J.'s relationship with Gladys was the complete opposite of the relationship he had with his mother. He considered Gladys an angel, and she looked upon him more as a son than a nephew. During those early years in her readings, Gladys asked Mr. Cayce about her past-life relationship with T.J. as in reading 288-45, T15:

(Q) What have been my past associations with the following individuals, what are the urges brought forth in the present, and how may I use them for our mutual development? First: Little nephew [1208?]:

(A) In those experiences in the land of the "city in the hills and the plains," and the effect as created by the activity of the entity through those periods which followed that.

For there we find the entity was the latent urge which brought about the ability for that entity to conquer the world, and never self! [See 1208-1 Reports.]

Then, as seen in the present experience of self as in relationships to same: These have brought and do bring material hardships, you see - physically manifested - yet in the mental and spiritual those influences which have been, may and will be wrought, in the shaping of the purposes, the desires, the hopes. All of these are coming within the realm of the entity's activities through the being willing for self to be effaced, that the greater force or influence of the entity's abilities may be made manifest in the present.

Recognizing the potential of this soul who was entrusted to her, Gladys doted on T.J., paying attention to everything the child did or said and then making a notation of it in his file in the archives. "I'm keeping a record of his 'sayings' which should be worth something some day if he turns out as we hope . . . ," she wrote when he was three. She would share them in subsequent letters to friends and family.

A letter to T.J.'s aunt Ruby in 1940, for instance, shared a story about T.J. that Gladys found amusing. "One afternoon we were coming back from the beach late, watching the moon and stars, etc. He said, 'Gladys, how did the moon get broken?' I tried to explain to him that it was not broken, but partly covered with a cloud. Then he asked, 'When will it get all boiled up like an egg?' I suppose he meant 'balled up' into a round moon. That same evening we met a boy coming from our house whom we had met previously on the beach and he had said he was *not* going to our house. Thos. Jeff. said, 'Well, you did go to our house, didn't you?' He said, 'Yes, I finally wound up there.' After he had gone on, Thos. Jeff. said to me, 'Gladys, how did he get all wound up?'"

Gladys made a notation of a conversation she had with T.J. on September 2, 1942. "As we were getting ready to leave the house this morning, Thos. Jeff. said, 'Gladys, may I take my bathing suit so I can go in swimming with that little boy and his mother at Muddie Cayce's house?' I said, 'I think it's too cold to go swimming, Thos. Jeff.' 'Oh, but Gladys,' he answered, 'It may warm *out.*'"

While these comments may not be out of the ordinary between a doting aunt and her young nephew, many of the talks these two souls had were anything but typical. As T.J. got older, Gladys told him about specific incidents in their past lives and would ask if he remembered this or that and he'd always say no. After all, he said, he was young and didn't pay much attention to specifics.

"Early on I didn't really care whether I knew someone in the past, unless I was having trouble with a relationship," he said, "and then Gladys would explain about a past life when she was there and why, karmically speaking, things were the way they were now."

When T.J. was six, Gladys wrote to Boyd who was overseas at the time, about a conversation she had with his son.

> TJ: "Aunt Gladys, when does Santa Claus die?"
> Gladys: "He doesn't die. Santa Claus is always alive."

TJ: "Why?"

Gladys: "Because Santa Claus is a spiritual being, like the angels."

TJ: "Well, Aunt Gladys, why can't we live always, like the angels and Santa Claus? Why do we have to die?"

Gladys: "Because we aren't good enough. If we always did good things and never bad things, we'd get so we could live all the time. Jesus was like that—He was so perfect that even when He was crucified He rose from the dead and kept right on living in the spirit plane and was the same as in the earth."

TJ: "Well, Aunt Gladys, that's not fair! It's not fair for Jesus and the angels and Santa Claus to live all the time, and we can't! Do you think if I was good all the time I'd live always?"

Gladys: "Of course—but you might not be able to do it in one lifetime. You know, even when you die you come back again and try to live better next time."

TJ: "I know it, Aunt Gladys, but it takes so long!"

T.J. spoke of their relationship as idyllic, saying she never raised her voice or became angry with him. Although she put almost all her energy into her work, according to T.J., she never brought it home. Their conversations were extraordinary—the kind you wished you could have been a fly on the wall so you could listen in.

"With Gladys I could always ask her opinion and she'd echo something Mr. Cayce said," he recalled. "She would even talk like Mr. Cayce. You could ask her questions and she'd answer, just like he did. Gladys had psychic abilities of her own, but she never talked about them or what she may have seen in a vision."

T.J. credited Gladys with an incredible memory. "My aunt Gladys told me once: 'I've always been with you in nearly every lifetime. We are tight. You and I, Mr. Cayce, and a couple of other people, we've always managed to be in the same neighborhood at least. The only time that I really couldn't take care of you was when I was the mother of Zend.' Zend was actually one of the lifetimes of Christ. It didn't bother me at all that I wasn't in that lifetime. I knew I was not up to that level yet, so I probably had been born in Czechoslovakia somewhere and I wasn't around during that lifetime. The other lifetimes, however, we were together, working in the same direction, trying to work out the 'we are one' thing."

Gladys liked to talk about T.J.'s lifetime as Sululon because she greatly helped him in that life. T.J. confided in her that he had some fears attached to the Alexander lifetime because of all the violence, but she explained karma to him and convinced him it wasn't always so dismal. She filled him in about his past lives like a TV reporter relaying a news story. She comforted him by saying that his purpose always has been to do good and that he was never alone—that she and Edgar Cayce had been with him for thousands of years.

Many years later when T.J. traveled through Central and South America, he had no idea that he followed an Atlantean trip he had taken thousands of years earlier until Gladys told him about it. While he was on that trip, he purchased swatches of cloth that he thought she'd like. After he gave them to her, it took her a year and a half to sew every one of those pieces of cloth on a blue jeans jacket for him, which he still has today.

"When Mr. Cayce was alive, I knew he and Gladys were both looking after me," he said. "It was comforting as a child to know that there were people watching out for you, especially ones who knew where you were all the time. That was total security. Gladys and Mr. Cayce were a team. No one was going to mess with me or take me away as long as they were there."

This was in stark contrast to the life he led when he was with one or both of his parents. Since they divorced when he was only five, he admits that remembering them as a couple is not easy except for isolated events here and there. Even so, living with them was not an ideal environment for a child.

"They both were heavily into the gambling business," T.J. said. "In those days, there was real gambling—not what you see in Las Vegas today. It didn't have anything to do with the bright lights and big-name performers. People had a real hunger to gamble and that hunger had nothing to do with show business. During the 1920s and 1930s, gambling and alcohol were against the law so everything was done underground. People would come to gamble at my mother's boyfriend's place on 17th Street called the 'O' Club. It extended about a half-block long over a grocery store and a waffle shop. They had roulette and dice games going on as well as horse betting. People would sit around drinking and talking to their friends. I could always tell who was doing well because if they drove a hot car like a Cadillac, they were winning a lot of money. If they drove an old pickup truck, they lost a lot of money."

Of course, alcohol was served at the club so when Burlynn did not have a sitter for him, he'd come along and be exposed to the drinking and gambling that went on around him. He remembered his mother taking him with her to another place called The Bandstand. Even though it wasn't a legal casino, he said it attracted prominent—and not so prominent—people in the community.

"There was gambling in the back of The Bandstand," he recalled. "On the outside was a beach bar and inside there were tables. Near the restroom there was a back door that opened into the rest of the place. That's where the gambling would take place. I was more interested in the music than anything else and there were always some musicians practicing."

According to T.J., there were quite a few casinos in Virginia Beach when he was a kid. He recalled that

Pacific Avenue had a trolley car that would stop at the train station and pick people up who were coming in from Washington, DC, Pennsylvania, or New York. They'd come in the summer and stay at the old inns, gamble, and then the bus would take them back. He learned to do his math in the bathrooms and his homework on the dice tables.

"Growing up, my friends were either people like Mr. Cayce and his friends who were totally out there, or all the undesirables in town I came to know through my parents."

Is it any wonder he preferred to live with his aunt Gladys?

Stability wasn't the only thing that Gladys provided her nephew. T.J. said he and Gladys were so close that they did not necessarily have to talk to each other because they always knew what the other was thinking. She enjoyed singing and she tried to cook, but T.J. did not consider cooking her best talent. He'd often go to the bowling alley up the street and have a burger rather than eat something she made—but this was more an endearment than an insult to her cooking. For the most part, they had this semi-normal "Leave it to Beaver" life, but with a little bit of a farm twist that included exotic chickens that would occasionally get loose and fly out. T.J. had to go and catch them on the Boardwalk. He laughed as he recalled how visitors would look at him as if he were crazy, running around, catching them, putting them in the sack, taking them home, and putting them back in the cage.

Animals were always a big part of T.J.'s life as a child. In a letter to T.J.'s father dated August 28, 1942, Gladys relayed the sad news about the passing of T.J.'s pet rabbit. "His little rabbit died one night not long ago, probably ate some poison grass, I don't know. A man was working around the place who is just crazy about Thos. Jeff. and he dug a grave . . . and Thos. Jeff. and the little boys down the street stood around with flowers in their hands to put on the grave. It was quite impressive. We talked a lot that night about the rabbit's spirit going to heaven and coming back in another baby rabbit sometime. He wanted to know if he couldn't attract him back to be his little rabbit again. I told him that since he hadn't taken very good care of the rabbit (I had to pick grass for him and tend to him entirely), perhaps the rabbit would prefer coming back to a little boy who appreciated him more. It is that part of his life that I'm going to miss so much."

To this day animals are drawn to him and he to them, being able to communicate with them fairly well. His property is a sanctuary for a variety of wildlife, including a home to a mother bear and her two now-grown cubs. When the cubs were little, mama bear would fall asleep under the pear tree and the cubs would scamper up the tree. Coyotes and possum come and walk around his front porch and there was a wild cat that called his place home as well. He reports that all the animals have been pretty friendly so far and they all seem to get along with each other. There are a number of feral cats on the property, and while none have been neutered, they never produce kittens. The animals just come and check him out. He has never bought an animal—they just seem to find him. People drop off their unwanted animals on the highway near his home, and the animals meander up his driveway and sit with him a spell.

After Gladys died, T.J. always felt she was nearby—still acting as his beloved guardian angel. When he was thinking about renting out half of the house that he had shared with her, he decided to ask her opinion first. He was conflicted because while he had a good job and made money at the Heritage Store, it was lonely living there without her. So he put it to her in spirit—did she think that was a good idea?

When he didn't hear anything from her, he went ahead and rented the front part of the house to Jim and Judy, a couple who worked with him at the Heritage Store. A few days after they moved in, Judy had an experience that frightened her. She ran to the back of the house where T.J. lived and started banging on his door, but when he wasn't there she went all over town looking for him. When he found this out, T.J. called her and asked what was wrong. She said she had been sitting in a chair close to what he described as a "little rinky-dink chandelier" that he had given Gladys and for no apparent reason, the lightbulb from the chandelier fell on her head. She was not hurt—more frightened than anything else—wondering how in the world a lightbulb could fall like that. There was no way to unscrew it without taking the fixture down first, so they came to the conclusion that it was a message from

Gladys.

Because of the extraordinary environment provided by Gladys and the Cayces, T.J. said he did not blame his mother for all the times she sent him away to be with Gladys. "You have to remember my mother's condition," he said in her defense. "It was so easy for her to just send me to Gladys. Many times she would pick me up for a little while, but I had to go to school, so I finally got to the point where I didn't see her at all for long periods and that was fine with me. If I had a choice, I preferred Gladys's company to living with my parents, hands down. While I was with my mother, I would complain that I wanted to go back to Gladys's house. I remember pestering her about it one time and she would just say, 'okay, fine.' When I was older, she'd put me on a Greyhound bus by myself to travel from my grandmother's house in Ohio to Virginia Beach."

Burlynn understood all about reincarnation, so she knew why T.J. wanted to go back to Gladys and the Cayces instead of staying with her. T.J. had no ill feelings about it and she knew that. In fact, he felt everyone knew that.

In May 1948, just a month shy of T.J.'s twelfth birthday, his mother remarried and after school was out, he went to live with her in Ohio. Gladys made a notation in his file that: "The marriage did not last very long and there was much moving around with many changes during the next two years, his most important 12th and 13th years."

As Gladys's notation said, T.J. and his family

moved around a lot. One of the clearer memories he has of his mother happened during a hurricane when they were living in Oceana. "My mother told me to stay upstairs while she went out with her girlfriend to find her car and move it," he recalled. "She had a watch that I always liked. She saw how scared I was so she gave me that watch to wear until she could get back. I weathered that hurricane alone."

Another of T.J.'s memories of his mother occurred when he was around thirteen. Burlynn and her friend Norma Jean decided to take a road trip to Phoenix and they took T.J. with them. He remembers they sat up front and drank beer while he was in the back, thinking about where they were going.

Before they got to Phoenix, the car broke down outside Tucumcari, New Mexico. It happened to be T.J.'s birthday, but he said it didn't matter because he believed Burlynn had forgotten all about that. The car needed a part at a gas station so they pulled in to this little town and found a place to stay.

"My mother told me I had to stay there and she and Norma Jean left," he recalled. "A Native American family owned the place. There was a man who sat out front on a bench looking as if Walt Disney put him together, complete with stovetop hat and blanket. He had a son my age that was out riding on his horse. The man asked me if I wanted to live there, thinking my mother had left me. I said my mother was coming back. He pointed to my cabin and said he'd leave me alone, but he came back a little later and knocked on the door. His son was with him and in a turn of synchronistic events, it happened to be the boy's birthday, too. Even though we were total strangers, we went off together and had a good time hanging out and eating his birthday cake."

T.J. added that later he went outside and started playing with what he believed to be a pack of about a dozen small dogs that were hanging around the cabin. He sat on the stoop and threw pieces of birthday cake to them. They were fighting each other for the cake, so he started talking to one of them and said, "Look, we have lots of cake so cool it!" They all sat down. The Native American elder started laughing. T.J. went in and got more cake and came out and fed them and then they all went off.

Burlynn and Norma Jean did not come back until the next day and when they did she apologized to her host. He looked at Burlynn and said, "Your son plays with coyotes and wolves." T.J. asked what he was talking about and he said that pack of dogs weren't dogs at all.

Once the car was repaired, they drove to Phoenix and stayed for a few days before returning to Burlynn's house in Virginia. T.J. stayed there for a few days until "things became out of control" and then he rode his bike back to Gladys's house.

As far as his father was concerned, T.J. said it did not bother him that they did not see each other for years on end because T.J. believed his father was working on his own karma.

"I didn't take it personally," he said. "It wasn't as

if my life were normal anyway. I was part of Mr. Cayce's plan. I wasn't Burlynn's son or Gladys's nephew. I was T.J. and until Mr. Cayce died, I followed the plan. Just because I was little did not mean anything to me. I knew I was part of this group that was going through time and space together. Until recently, I never fully realized how much I really loved Mr. Cayce and my aunt Gladys. After all, they were the only family I knew. If it hadn't been for Mr. Cayce's knowledge of reincarnation and everything else that he knew, I never would have ended up there. I would have stayed with my parents. Given their circumstances in life, I was fortunate indeed to have been plucked out of Boyd and Burlynn's house and dropped in the loving arms of the Cayces and my aunt Gladys."

Gladys's last day in the Edgar Cayce Foundation office was December 31, 1985. She had been to a doctor, thinking she had a gum infection, complaining she felt tired and worn out. Several days later, Dr. O. M. Wakefield, a longtime friend and family doctor, diagnosed her condition as acute leukemia and admitted her to Virginia Beach General Hospital. Knowing the seriousness of her condition and its eventual outcome, she did not want any heroic measures. Despite how ill she was, her focus remained on "the Work," commenting: "Well, even if I do die from this whatever it is, I'm just going right back to work."

Gladys died on February 12, 1986, at 10:00 p.m. T.J. was not present at the time of her death, but she has never left him, continuing to be his guardian angel every day of his life.

Chapter Fourteen

T.J.'s Past Lives

It wasn't unusual for Edgar Cayce to tell someone that they had a famous past life, just as it wasn't unusual for him to tell them they had been a John Doe or a Plain Jane. But let's face it. If you had a famous past life and were plagued by issues in this lifetime, wouldn't it make sense to seek out the one man who wouldn't sugar coat anything but be straight with you about who you were, what you did, and why you're here?

T.J. remembers many people who had a famous past life or two who came to live at the Cayce home. There were some rather unbelievable souls who came and went all the time. Many would come to Virginia Beach and ask Cayce to help them out of a dire illness while others would just come to help with "the Work." Everybody in the house knew everybody else's past lifetime. T.J. believes that's why they tolerated him and were always patting him on the head.

So now imagine what it was like for T.J. to be born into a situation where he's living in a house where reincarnation is talked about all the time, as if there was no doubt about its validity whatsoever. No one ever told him that there was no such thing as past lives. On the contrary, from a very young age he was aware that as a soul you come and go, come and go, and you try to get better each time. That was his reality. There was no way he could deny it because he was there and he saw many examples of what it was like to be in another dimension. So, from his childlike perspective, all things were possible.

Watching all these people come to Cayce's home, T.J. learned early on that souls tended to reincarnate together. As they interacted, it was obvious to T.J. that this wasn't the first time they had been together. He said he was always open to this reality and that was why he was glad to meet people he knew before. Even though he may not have the chance to get to know them very well in this life, having the opportunity to meet them again made him happy.

Cayce gave T.J. four past lives in his life reading, but like any other soul, he had countless more than the four Cayce shared. For instance, even though he did not tell T.J. that he had a past life in Egypt, T.J. knew he was alive at the time of Cayce's incarnation as Ra Ta when the pyramids were being built.

"Mr. Cayce would talk about the pyramids and then shoot back to a lifetime in Atlantis, which we also shared, if something reminded him about that incarnation," said T.J. "We never discussed past lives in chronological order because he did not see time and space in a linear way."

In regard to the four past lives that Edgar Cayce gave him in his life reading, T.J. said: "I do not now, nor have I ever, gone around claiming to have been any of the four men he identified in my life reading, but having come from Mr. Cayce, I have accepted these identities as true. Nonetheless, I have a hard time saying their names out loud. I'd rather say I was Brer Rabbit."

Cayce gave T.J. the four incarnations that he felt were relevant to this lifetime. This was a common number of past lives given in any one life reading. Edgar would have given him more had he lived to give that second life reading, but that did not happen, so these four are the primary ones T.J. has been working on. There is a common denominator that runs through each of them that has given T.J. information he needs for this life, yet without that second reading, he has felt as though he's missing some valuable and essential pieces.

Sululon in Atlantis

The first lifetime Edgar told T.J. about was one he shared with him in Atlantis that occurred around the time of the continent's destruction.

The entity then took the part of those who later became the heads of those that warred against those of the Law of One, and then in the name of Sululon—as would be termed in the present.

In those experiences the entity made for destructive forces in the early experiences, yet with those activities that brought about the union in body with one of the daughters of the Law of One, the entity then become to each group as one set apart. For the teachers of the Law of One were afraid of the ability, while those that were of the sons of Belial were afraid of the entity becoming what would be termed in the present as a traitor.

Hence throughout those periods the entity became then *that one* that led the first establishing of the activity in the varied lands that came to be known as later the Mayan, the Yucatan, the Inca, the Peruvian – and *later* the Mound Builders in the northern portions of the entity's present sojourn. [Ohio?]

Not that the entity remained there, but

established those activities which has become a part of the entity by those divisions (1208-1, T29–32).

From what he knows of this lifetime, T.J. said Sululon initially led a dark existence at a time when the Atlantean people were divided. "There were the Sons of Belial (the bad guys) and the Children of the Law of One (the good guys)—who were also known as the Sons of Light and the Daughters of Light," he explained. "These poor souls had nothing, but they were creative people who wanted nothing more than to keep Atlantis together. They knew that God was love.

"The Sons of Belial were materialistic and selfish, somewhat like corrupt corporations and greedy banks are today—only worse. They were miserable people who took advantage of everyone. They just wanted to take everything. Atlantis was about to fall apart. The vibrations of the earth were awful because there was so much misuse of power. It is very similar to today, only the Atlantean weapons were bad news. They used lasers to cut up the earth, shooting all over the place, killing people. Things were falling out of the sky. It was a really dangerous time to be alive.

"Sululon was a leader of the Sons of Belial, getting whatever he could for himself. His primary interest was in ripping off people and getting all the money and power he could amass. He knew what was going on and that Atlantis was in real trouble. After all, his people partially were responsible for why Atlantis fell apart, but he had no idea they had so screwed it up to the point where it totally would disappear.

"But then something happened to turn me away from the Sons of Belial and become part of the Law of One," he said. "I met a woman who was an early incarnation of my aunt Gladys. I recognized her as someone I had known forever. We fell in love, and I understood for the first time what love really was. She turned me around and I changed, and that's when I started to feel guilty. I knew what was in store for Atlantis, and I felt responsible for its demise. I confided this to her and she convinced me that we needed to get people out of there before the continent was destroyed. So I joined forces with the Law of One."

According to T.J., the Sons of Belial now looked upon him as a traitor and wanted to kill him. The soul that was Gladys continued to urge him to leave with her and take as many people with them as possible. And that's what they did.

"Mr. Cayce said I got together a group of souls," he said. "I don't know how many, but there must have been a lot of them. I told them to grab everything they had. We barely got out of there by the skin of our teeth. We looked much like a caravan crisscrossing the earth. As we went along, we would drop people off and say— okay, you live here; you live there. In that way, I helped settle the Incas, the Aztecs, the Peruvians, and the Mound Builders. They began civilizations. Mr. Cayce was helpful in showing how to build all those pyramids."

T.J. said that when a group of people gathered on the porch outside of Hugh Lynn's office at the old hospital building, the favorite topic of conversation was Atlantis and earth changes. T.J. studied the Atlantean civilization fairly well in this life—sometimes out of boredom, but other times because it was exciting to hear what those people could do. He always had a real interest in Atlantis; wanting to understand what went wrong.

"That information is important for us to know because what went on in Atlantis is happening right here, right now," he stated. "I feel that we are long overdue for these earth changes."

While he considers his life as Sululon as one in which he did not do well in the beginning, he believes in the end, through Gladys's intervention, his change of heart created enormous good and that, in turn, resolved a lot of that lifetime's karma.

Donquiellen in France

The next lifetime Cayce gave T.J. occurred in the early history of France, when the Normans and Britons dominated that country. His name was Donquiellen and Edgar said T.J. was there to put a government together, which is basically the same government France has today.

> The experience before that we find was in those periods when there were the disturbances in or the establishing of that

land now called France, when there were the first of the separations through the Gallic Wars, through the activities that made for a separation for the east or for the west portions of the Helvetic activities— the Romans and Britons and the Normans. [Yrs. 200–100 B.C.?]

The entity then was among those that made for the establishing or the setting of this apart in those periods of the experience, in the name then Donquiellen.

In the experience the entity gained and lost. Gained, and through those activities brought into the influences of those peoples that which has remained much of the basic forces of that as a nation, that as a people, that has been as a *separate* influence in the affairs of the world throughout the periods since that establishment (1208-1, T21–23).

T.J. and I both searched for information on Donquiellen to no avail. Consequently we know nothing about him, other than what is in the reading. T.J. has chosen not to explore this—or any other lifetime—through past-life regression—so he can't offer any perspective based on memory or bleed through. However, if in fact Donquiellen was instrumental in putting the government of France together, we can see how that life influenced the future author of the Declaration of Independence.

While Sululon and Donquiellen may be obscure characters in history, T.J.'s next two lifetimes are the ones he has the most trouble discussing, because they were both famous lives. T.J. is an avid reader and says that in almost every book he gravitates to, these two men's names are mentioned. He muses that perhaps it's a cosmic joke, but nonetheless, he finds it annoying!

Alexander the Great

Before that we find the entity was in that land during those periods when there were the activities that made for the rise and fall of many lands, in the Grecian, the Persian, all of the eastern lands; when *that* entity now known as Alexander the Great made for the conquering forces of the earth—the depleting that there might bring to self the exaltations [356–323 B.C.].

Here the entity lost. For these will become in the experience of the entity those influences that might makes for right, or power making for indulgences. And if these are not conquered in the experiences as the principles that are set in its earthly experience, these may run as wild in the very activities of the entity—even as then (1208-1, T26–27).

"People know pretty much what he did but from my perspective, I don't think the word 'Great' applies to his lifetime at all," T.J. said. "Everyone knows about his army going around conquering nations and killing people. Frankly, I don't know what to think of Alexander, except to shiver whenever it comes up because I know I earned some bad karma there. I acquired some bad karma during my stint in the Marine Corps in this life, but nowhere at the level of this guy."

T.J. added that ever since he was a child, it freaked him out to know he had actually killed people in a past life. "I don't kill anything," he said. "If I see any creatures crawling on the driveway, I pick them up. One day I spent a half hour taking all the little tadpoles out of my neighbor's driveway because I didn't want him to run them over."

T.J. said that for most of his life he labored under the assumption that many of his karmic difficulties with specific individuals came from actions he took against them in Alexander's lifetime. This was based on things people told him—not events he actually remembered. Once he found out that historically those stories were inaccurate, he felt tremendous relief.

"This isn't to say I did not have any memories of being Alexander," he said. "Even when you adamantly deny a specific past life, occasionally scenes present themselves in your mind as a memory, not as your imagination. A few of those came into my mind about Alexander."

For example, T.J. remembers once phoning Gladys and telling her about a book he had just read on Alexander. In her notes about that conversation, she wrote that T.J. could "... *remember* the incidents of Alexander's childhood—in fact, some of these things have come out in his dreams during the last year or so." Apparently that book triggered some bleed through of that lifetime.

T.J. also cannot deny that he felt drawn to Greece and can only surmise that it was because of Alexander's lifetime there. The yearning was so great that in September 1970 he announced he wanted to spend the winter in Greece.

"I've had several experiences in dreams which make me know I must go," he wrote. "For a long time I've been complaining about conditions of the world and the so-called 'establishment.' Now I've come to realize that I personally was responsible for starting much that has come to pass. So, I must go back over there where it all started and see if I can find myself."

T.J. says he tends not to feel too good about himself because he realizes he has a lot to pay for in light of Alexander's actions in his brief, but very powerful, lifetime.

"He only lived to thirty-three," T.J. said of Alexander. "When I passed thirty-three in this lifetime, I felt as if I had a reprieve. No matter what I do in this lifetime, I can't give myself too much of a pat on the back because when I look back on Alexander's life, I say: 'Okay, those were my decisions then so I need to be on my best behavior now.'"

One of the lessons Cayce taught young T.J. was that there was value in knowing who you had been in a previous life, if for no other reason than to know that when you first encounter a person that you have strong feelings about, you realize that your relationship is what it is now because of what it was before and in some cases, you need some protection. That was certainly the case with T.J.'s relationship with many of the people he encountered later in life.

Thomas Jefferson

The final lifetime Cayce gave T.J. is the one that is his namesake, Thomas Jefferson. Whenever T.J. says that out loud in public, he waits a few minutes for people to snicker. He doesn't blame them if they do.

Before this, as given, the entity lived in the earth during those periods when there were the turmoils in that known as the Revolution, and in the activities of the Colonists.

The entity then, as Thomas Jefferson, made these contributions to the activities of the people—that are well known, or may be had through the many references that may be drawn upon by those seeking to know [Yrs. 1743–1826].

But rather seek to know the *basic forces* that *directed* same. For the inventive genius that *prompted* the activities of the entity then, the curious nature that made for the many oppositions that arose in the experience, are those things that are indicated in the two natures that apparently will be in the developing period of the entity's activities.

Hence in the application of same, not because of "*he was*" but because these may be *used*, there should be the correct guidance and training in his formative years. For as a great landowner will the entity be if it reaches the years of its majority (1208-1, T17–20).

T.J. has had a hard time with the Jefferson life for many reasons, not the least of which is the fact that he lives in an old farmhouse on land that extends upward all the way to the top of his "little mountain." The first week he was there, T.J. decided to go exploring. When he got to the top of the property, he looked over and realized he had a clear view of Monticello.

"My mountain was about the same size as my former property and sat almost directly across from it," he said. "I took out my binoculars to get a better look and saw all these people milling around. Looking across at Monticello became a real headache for me, and consequently I stopped going up there. Besides, the trees have grown so tall now that I can't clearly see Monticello anymore and it's just as well."

It's been nothing short of miraculous that T.J. has been able to hold on to his property. Jefferson continued to borrow until he died bankrupt.

"I still don't have any money, but I have this great piece of property," he says. "I may have fulfilled Mr. Cayce's prediction that I'd be a great landowner, but like Mr. Jefferson, I still can't afford to pay my taxes!"

T.J. was once asked whether he believes he was Thomas Jefferson because of his own memories, or because Cayce told him he had been Jefferson. While he usually says it's the latter, as with the Alexander lifetime, there have been occasions in his life when "memories" have bubbled to the surface when he least expected, starting at the age of three.

In a January 5, 1939, letter, Edgar Cayce revealed T.J.'s ability to recall the Jefferson lifetime. "We had a quiet Xmas as H.L. didn't get home until the 27th—of course we had a tree for Thos. Jeff—the sharpest kid I ever saw—not believable—but he repeated part of the Declaration for me a few days ago—insists he wrote it."

Gladys noted shortly after T.J.'s third birthday that he was a "determined little fellow," that he was "always trying to change the subject if you go to correct him about anything, but he doesn't want anybody changing the subject on him!"

The people who were watching T.J. grow up looked for signs of his Jefferson past life to manifest. In April 1943, on the occasion of Jefferson's 200th birthday, Mrs. (#2072) wrote wondering what T.J.'s reaction was to this momentous occasion. Considering T.J. was only six, it's doubtful he had any reaction to it at all. Mrs. (#2072) commented about the article that appeared in *Life* magazine on April 12 (Jefferson's birthday is April 13), which featured a portrait of Jefferson done by Charles Wilson Peale in 1791. She wrote, "It seemed to me I could see so much likeness, in the eyes and set of mouth especially. Hardly have I ever *seen* so much proof of reincarnation. Give me a strange sort of feeling."

Apparently many people at the A.R.E. were aware of this particular past life. Cayce received a letter from [#1837], who obviously was thinking about T.J.

> Yesterday, when I was selecting books to be sold at a home of a sick friend . . . I found two volumes published in 1829, *Memoirs Correspondence* and *Miscellaneous of Thomas Jefferson* bound in morocco, and I wondered if Miss [288]'s brother [391] would like to keep them for the son [1208].

I was so intrigued when you told me about him and I met the boy. These volumes are doubtless rare and long out of print. In one is a facsimile of the original draft of the Declaration of Independence. A friend, whom I took to see all the books, wanted these volumes (for a pittance) but he agreed with me that they might have a real value for either a collector or some one especially interested in Jefferson. So I thought of the little [1208] boy and your reading for him at birth, and asked Mr. Wadsworth to hold them till I could hear from you. In the meantime I am writing to a dealer in rare books, to learn their value.

Cayce was grateful for her offer and said he'd like to get the volumes on Thomas Jefferson for Gladys and that he was willing to pay for them. She responded saying that she had packed the volumes to mail to him and added, "I'm sure the little [1208] boy will prize them when he is older." T.J. does not remember ever seeing these books and has no idea what became of them.

The first time T.J. visited Monticello in this life was when he was sixteen. The father of a friend of his was a navy chaplain and when he was in port, he wanted to take his son to Charlottesville to check out the University of Virginia. T.J. tagged along. The trip took all day because there were no interstate highways then and they had to travel on Route 60 the whole way.

T.J. wrote a letter to his mother telling her of the experience: "A few friends and I drove up to Charlottesville on a little trip last Monday to see Monticello. We saw his [Jefferson]'s home and where he was buried. That's where I want to go to college—the University of Virginia."

Years ago the tours at Monticello weren't as sophisticated as they are today. During one of his visits he walked in and the docent asked his name, to which he replied, "Thomas Jefferson."

"Are you related to Thomas Jefferson?" she asked.

"Well, indirectly," T.J. answered sheepishly.

"Well, you get to go upstairs if you're a relative and check out the top room."

"I've been up there before, don't worry about it," he replied.

But she insisted he go up and hang out for a while. So he did, following the narrow stairway that leads upstairs.

"The Templars and Masons probably met there to draw up their strategy," he said. "Honestly, I thought it was really boring. They had a few statues around the window but that's about it. I stayed for a little while and then I left."

His last visit occurred several years ago. He said that every once in a while he wanted to see what good things he did in the past so he could feel better about himself. He tells how he drove to Monticello on the 4th of

July when they host their annual naturalization ceremony for new citizens. There wasn't anywhere to park. The attendant came up and told T.J. that he was sorry, but he would not be able to watch the program because there were no parking places left, to which T.J. replied, "Man, my name is Thomas Jefferson. You're not going to let me come in and look at this?"

"I'm sorry, Mr. Jefferson, we can't let you in here today," the attendant responded.

T.J. thought—"You idiot. This is my house!" Of course, not wanting to get locked up in a mental institution, he refrained from saying that out loud.

Even after Edgar was gone, T.J. said his mentor continued to send messages about him to those closest to him. In May 1954, Burlynn told of an incident in which Mr. Cayce appeared and confirmed T.J.'s past-life identity.

"The other night I was standing by the sink and I was alone," Burlynn wrote. "Edgar Cayce came up behind me and I turned around. He went over to the kitchen table and sat down in one of the chairs beside it. He looked at me very intently and said, 'Don't worry – He *is* Thomas Jefferson.' Then he came back over, looked down at me and smiled. Then he was gone. The kitchen got real chilly after that and then I got the willies, you might call it. I thought, was he here or did I dream it? But it did happen..."

This fascination for the Jefferson lifetime did not end when T.J. grew up. In 1978, he wrote a letter to his sixteen-year-old son who was asking for advice. T.J. shared some life lessons with his son.

Hello [#1 son], I was glad to get your letter and am flattered that you would seek my advice. So, here are my ideas on a subject I am not strange to. For one thing, indiscriminately eating drugs that you *know* very little about is a *danger*. It does sometimes start as a game. However, drugs are quite real and quite serious. So, don't be fooled by the "hemes" (people) who "laugh it off." I know it's for real because real people I have known have ended in an O.D. (overdose) and quite *dead* literally! Thinking all along a *game* of chicken. A person's body is not a replaceable toy. It *is* your vehicle for life on this planet. Take *care* of it. There are lots of flashes to be had on lots of different levels. The thing is not to jump into anything you aren't sure of. Know your limitations. Speed is real dumb but shooters are a sad and lonely trip. However, this subject is better discussed in person. Maybe we will get the chance soon. Just understand that artificial flashes from drugs isn't really such a big part of life. Don't feel like you have missed out on anything especially good. Your "friend" who said "Don't knock it 'til you've tried it" should know that that is one of the most asinine sayings ever invented. That's like saying "Don't knock scarlet fever 'til you've tried it" - or hard times, or confusion, etc. Don't fall game to a fool's ploy, [...] [Son], or reassure them that what they are doing is all right by joining in. Deep inside you know what is right. *Make* the time to sit quietly and get to know your feelings. Space out a little on the subject—it helps to clear the mind, you know. Feelings will always tell you right from wrong for you, if you learn how to cut through all the illusions; meaning other people's hang-ups and your own. (Everybody has hang-ups; the object is to try to master them instead of letting them master you). See through to the *truth*. There is a lesson to be learned almost everywhere you turn. It is my feeling that it hasn't been learned until you feel good about your decisions—at that point you become a leader of good leadership. One of the fine tricks of life is how to enjoy. How can you have a good time, even at a party, if you are not enjoying life? A sense of humor is essential. If you can see it through a sense of humor you are not, or can't be, all bad. Another trick is to enjoy some little things; like walking from one place to another—some sunshine, a cold glass of milk, etc. The point is that it is all the little things that, bunched together, make up your life. *If* you take pleasure in all these little things, life as a whole will be more enjoyable. Being sincerely happy *deep down* is where the best highs are. Learning how to get the real thing is much more of a challenge than a quick flash, that is as easy as taking a pill—Big Deal! Hang in there and listen to *your* self, not a bunch of people that you will not even remember what their faces look like in ten years. Life is a trip and yours is in its beginning. You have lots of hours to live. Spend your *time* wisely—it's more, *more* precious than money. When you run out of money you can get more. Needless to say, when you run out your time—it's just gone! Soon you will be on your own, so try for as much positive learning as you can. Try not to do anything you will regret later. Know your limitations. This letter was composed unitarily by [GD's note: His 3rd wife] and me; hope it is a help. Advice is not cheap if it comes from the experience. Hang in there, man. Love, Dad ([1208]) and [...] P.S. Nice paper, huh?

Gladys copied the letter for T.J.'s file and made a notation that she had shared the letter with her husband, Les, who said: "Well, for the first time he sounds to me like Thomas Jefferson." Somehow T.J. just could never get away from that kind of past-life scrutiny.

Because his approach to life was based on what Cayce taught him, T.J. found school boring in comparison. Consequently, he'd spend most of his time staring out the window and thinking about things that weren't of this world. When he was a freshman in high school, he kept thinking that the world was going to end. He was lonely and wasn't doing that well in school.

At the end of the year, he was given a history exam and he couldn't answer any of the questions. Part of the problem was that he thought the questions were inconsequential and felt his teacher should be asking something more profound. Nonetheless, he knew he would fail if he didn't do well on this test.

"My teacher had already warned me that if I failed, I'd have to repeat that year and that was the last thing I wanted to do," he said. "I didn't want what few friends I had to laugh at me. So I sat there for about five minutes and thought—well, I have to write something. So I opened myself up to the Universe and without realizing it, began writing out the entire Declaration of Independence and the Statute for Religious Freedom for Virginia. I signed about eight signatures, including John Adams and a few other guys I liked from that lifetime. It just came to me, totally out of the blue. It didn't freak me out because I could do things like that. If I could see colors around people and trees, and then see fairies in the garden, pretty much anything was possible after that."

He gave the paper to his teacher and said, "That's all I know about history. You can pass or fail me."

Looking at the paper, she was furious and told T.J. she had had enough of him, calling his response "ridiculous."

T.J. agreed with her. For him it was ridiculous because no matter how many schools he went to in one year, whenever he attended classes on different subjects, he'd end up saying—"That's not the way it was."

"You can't tell a teacher 'that's not how it was' and then start talking about Atlantis," he said. "You can imagine the reputation I had. The other kids didn't want to be around me."

After reading his paper, T.J.'s teacher didn't know what to say, so he was suspended while the staff investigated how he managed to write those two documents word for word. They couldn't come up with a reasonable explanation because he was sitting in front of his teacher the whole time. She couldn't very well say he cheated because no one else knew what he was writing, so finally she promoted him to tenth grade.

T.J.'s troubles in school did not dampen his appetite for learning. The fact that Thomas Jefferson attended William & Mary and began a career as a lawyer may have had both a conscious and subconscious influence on T.J. Writing to his mother in 1957 while he was on the high seas, he reflected on his academic career.

"Seems like everything I ever did I completed only by the skin of my teeth," he wrote. "That, my dear mother, will cease. When I start college I will have prepared myself to such an extent that there will be no stoppers or detours. I'm going straight to the top. I will be the greatest thing in law since ole Thomas Jefferson himself."

Four years later, Gladys noted that T.J. started a correspondence course in law with LaSalle University Extension and was doing very well on his tests, but it was hard to find the required ten hours a week to spend on it and he eventually gave up.

While the Jefferson life had many lofty accomplishments, the fact that Jefferson owned slaves is an issue that to this day haunts T.J. Evidence of how this past-life remnant impacted his life first surfaced when he was a young boy of six. Gladys, who was especially in tune with seeing signs of the Jefferson lifetime in T.J., wrote to his father on August 8, 1942, about an incident she witnessed.

"I certainly can see his Reading in him," she wrote, "or the characteristics mentioned in his Life Reading; for instance, he regards all people alike. Walking down the street the other day he was right behind [an African-American] boy who had on a big sailor hat, or the kind worn in the tropics—I don't know the name of it. So immediately he wanted the boy to give him the hat, or to let him wear it; no thought at all of superiority. In fact he walked the whole block ahead of me right along side the boy, talking to him about everything under the sun."

T.J. was greatly influenced by Gladys's first husband, Al Turner, who was active in the civil rights movement. T.J. remembered that when he was a child, Gladys and Al opened their home to one of the leaders of the Virginia chapter of the NAACP (National Association for the Advancement of Colored People) who held meetings there. T.J. said they had to keep that man hidden and that sometimes they would have to drive him home in the middle of the night so they'd be safe under the cover of darkness.

When T.J. was older, he decided he wanted to join the NAACP. By then the group was meeting in Norfolk. One night T.J. rode his motorbike to Norfolk to join up. He recalled the look on their faces when he walked in the door.

"Someone finally asked me what I wanted and I said I was there to join," he said. "They smiled and said, 'Well, sit down and fill this out.' I believe I was the first white kid in Virginia Beach to join the NAACP. I am very proud of that."

T.J.'s commitment to the organization continued into adulthood. A notation in his file reflects that. "Aunt [288] reported that although deeply in debt from installment buying, and payments on an expensive foreign sports car which he doesn't want to give up, he nevertheless felt it important recently to pay the fee for becoming a member of the NAACP."

It seemed to Gladys that T.J. came into this life

with a built-in sensitivity to prejudice, which must have been a real challenge for a child of the South. Since half of the relatives on his father's side of the family were from Selma, Alabama, T.J. said he had to deal with their prejudices and "twisted ideas" about God.

"When the riots were happening in Selma, it drove me crazy," he said. "I could not understand why they were doing this. Couldn't they understand we were all created at the same time? Those were the kinds of thoughts that would hit me—that we're not different. The Arabs and Jews—none of us are different. We all had the same start."

Another tie-in to the Jefferson life occurred when T.J. first moved to the Charlottesville area and lived at Lake Monticello in Fluvanna County. Several times a week he would drive in to town on Route 20, which at one point parallels Jefferson Vineyards. At the curve of the road there was a little stone country store where T.J. would park his truck and sit and have coffee.

It was at that store that he met Lou Hatch, who worked there at the time. Her husband, Peter Hatch, was managing the gardens at Monticello. Lou and T.J. became friends because their children were the same age and went to the same school. At that point T.J. was trying to earn a living because he was a stay-at-home dad. He decided to sell vegetables and herbs to people so he started a small business he called Jefferson's Garden Farm and he'd sell herbs to places like Keswick Hall.

Eventually T.J. asked Lou if she thought Peter would hire him to work in the garden at Monticello.

By then, T.J. also had become friends with Gabrielle Rausse, an Italian winemaker who established Jefferson Vineyards. T.J. had an interest in wine making, which was not surprising, considering Jefferson is considered America's "first distinguished viticulturist" and "the greatest patron of wine and wine growing that this country has yet had." During his lifetime, Jefferson established two vineyards at Monticello, but neither was successful. Today, the vineyard that is his namesake is thriving and producing award-winning wines. It's no wonder Rausse and T.J. became friends.

"Gabrielle liked me because I had gone to school and traveled throughout Italy and I could speak a little Italian," T.J. recalled. "He also liked it that my name was Thomas Jefferson. I told him I was interested in wine making, especially at Monticello, so he invited me to come out to the vineyards on weekends and watch the operation. I never did work there and I never did get the job at Monticello. By the time I connected with Peter again, it was winter, so I didn't pursue it after that."

Synchronistic events involving Jefferson happen to T.J. all the time. Someone once sent him a catalog of reproductions of Thomas Jefferson's belongings on display at Monticello. Since he had just moved into his house and didn't have any furniture, he looked through the catalog and selected a dozen things. Monticello had a warehouse on Route 250 where you could buy duplicates of these items, so T.J. went over there and bought quite a few pieces. He later learned that the things he bought were replicas of items that Jefferson loved the most.

One of the stories that T.J. tells is yet another example of how T.J. had continued reminders of the Jefferson life. This particular incident happened on April 13, 1993, the 150th birthday of Thomas Jefferson and two years after the fall of the Soviet Union. Mikhail Gorbachev, the last Soviet premier, came to Charlottesville. He visited the University of Virginia and then found himself in the home of a man he claimed greatly influenced him— Thomas Jefferson. His motorcade was tying up traffic in the area just at the time T.J. had to go to Monticello High School to pick up one of his daughters. He knew how to get around the traffic by taking side roads.

"So I'm coming down a little feeder road and the motorcade is coming along next to me. There was this long, black limousine with police cars and motorcycles everywhere and the lights flashing. I'm stuck there waiting, getting nervous because I think I'm going to be late to get my daughter, and all of a sudden the window rolls down and it's Gorbachev sitting there in the seat. I looked at him.

"Mr. Gorbachev, how are you?" I yelled across the road.

"Fine. What's your name?"

"Thomas Jefferson."

"Nice to meet you, Mr. Jefferson."

T.J. said that was as close to diplomatic relations as he got in this lifetime.

For those who believe in reincarnation, the fact

that the soul that was Thomas Jefferson has reincarnated in our time has propelled him to the status of a rock star. All of his life, people have been intrigued by what he had to say or what he would do. It may surprise people to know that it's his connection to Edgar Cayce, and not his past life as Jefferson, that he feels is the more compelling story.

"If you were to ask me what was more important to me—believing as Mr. Cayce said that I was Thomas Jefferson, or having had those years growing up in the Cayce household, I would say without question it was the time I spent with Mr. Cayce," T.J. said. "However, the fact that he said I had been Jefferson is of endless fascination to people who get more caught up in that than they do in the global outreach of the Cayce readings. When I gave talks to A.R.E. groups, what I loved the most about those talks was that the people there were more interested in what I remembered about Mr. Cayce than in what the former Thomas Jefferson had to say about the mess we're in today. As much as I try to downplay my past lives, they continue to come up, especially with individuals who insist they knew me in that lifetime."

T.J. believes that the need to sensationalize past lives is something only people who have not had the burden of a famous past life want to perpetuate. From his experience, it is difficult to reconcile a famous past life to the life one is leading now. He readily admits he is not the idol that so many people believe him to be, but he also admits he benefited from people believing he had been

Jefferson. One of those people was Chinese Arhatic Yoga Master Choa, under whom T.J. studied for eight years.

"When I hooked up with Master Choa, he was really big on looking at auras," T.J. explained. "I was so skeptical. The first time I went to see him give a talk, he could tell I thought he was full of it because I never met anybody like Mr. Cayce. So when somebody tells me they can see auras, I go—whoa! I want to see why. So he had me stand up and someone in back of me said he would catch me and I fell on my butt. I felt a force come to me and hit me right in the chest and I couldn't believe it and I was hooked. It was just like levitating. I was hooked on Mr. Cayce when he did all these things and this man, Master Choa, could do a lot of stuff similar to Cayce. A lot of his work was in colors. He was a healer and he would look at a person's body and he'd find the colors would change by the second. If he found an area where someone was sick or lacking in something, he could heal that with color and energy. I hadn't tried to see auras in a long time and it's still really difficult, but I'm still able to see them around trees and bushes without a problem."

But even with Master Choa, T.J. could not escape his past life as Jefferson, admitting that one of the reasons Master Choa liked him was because of the Jefferson lifetime.

"I never told him about that past life," T.J. admitted. "But one day in one of his lectures he asked me to stand up. He said he wanted to thank me personally because if it hadn't been for religious freedom, he wouldn't have been able to come here and have this course."

As a result of his notoriety, T.J. got a lot of free perks during his eight-year association with Master Choa. "I never had to pay for anything," he admitted. "He'd give me everything for free. He would pay for my hotel room and we would go on shopping sprees."

It wasn't until high school that T.J. truly understood who Alexander or Jefferson were in a historical context, adding that looking back, he didn't feel it was wise for anyone to tell him as a child that he had been both of those men.

"Imagine, you have a kid and you tell him, 'You were Alexander the Great and you were Thomas Jefferson.' I had no chance at a real life. Add to this that in this life I didn't even have a name when I showed up at Mr. Cayce's house, and he goes and names me Thomas Jefferson. If someone else in my family had named me, I would have been really arrogant and angry. But Mr. Cayce did it, and he was never wrong about anything. So, there I was living again in Virginia with the name Thomas Jefferson, so right from birth I had a lot to contend with."

As he grew older, T.J. learned to live with the notion that he had been Jefferson and Alexander, but it was the other information Cayce put in his reading that has haunted him ever since—the idea that in this life he could do for the world what Jefferson did for the United States. He feels he may have been able to deal with that better had he had the life reading Cayce promised when he turned thirteen. ["When the entity has passed its thirteenth year, begin again" (1208-1, T35)].

"But he died before that happened," T.J. repeated, "and I was left thinking—well, wait a minute. What about this? What's the next act? Where do I go with what I know? Mr. Cayce said some pretty fantastic things about what I could do if I put my mind to it. I felt he set me up knowing this; that I could do this and that, but I was left thinking—Mr. Cayce, you're not here anymore to guide me and I'm only nine years old."

T.J. says his life hasn't been easy because the load that he carries is huge—trying to be a "normal" human being on the one hand and being faced with the way he was raised at the Cayce house on the other.

"The factors of my upbringing put me in one dimension here, one dimension there," he said. "It wasn't because of something I read in a book or believe or thought, but something that I was part of and saw on a personal level. I knew Mr. Cayce was getting his information about past lives from the Akashic Records and as a child, I asked him several times what the place looked like. He said it was a big hall that you go into and look something up, just as you would in a library. We don't have anybody now who can do that as well as Mr. Cayce, but we have all his readings. What kind of question could I possibly come up with that I couldn't find in those fourteen thousand readings?"

T.J. has focused almost his entire life on what he did wrong. While it is constantly in his peripheral vision, he never thought that was a bad thing. For him it has been helpful. For instance, when he examines his life reading, he reflects on the principle that anyone can turn his life around as he did in his Atlantean lifetime by choosing to follow the Law of One and thereby embracing love and the awareness of our oneness.

"The four past lives that he said I had were all people who saw a problem and tried to fix it," he said. "I sometimes really botched up the job, but there were a few times I did okay. Nonetheless, there are people who criticize me because they feel I never lived up to Mr. Cayce's prediction of what I could do. I've felt guilty about that all my life, but I don't want to hear it's my fault anymore. It is much too complicated for the blame to be placed on me based on what I did in a past life, or what Mr. Cayce saw I could do if—and it's a big if—I was raised in a certain way. At such a young age, I could not make those decisions for myself and by the time I was old enough to understand the magnitude of what was on my shoulders, I was so lost that I did not have the strength or the wherewithal to turn my life around. Now when I think in terms of whether I am okay with myself, I can honestly say that I am. Sure, I've done a lot of things that I could have done better but I have also done a lot of things better than I used to, so I see progress in myself to the point where I am happy about it. If I'm the last human standing, at least I know why I'm here."

Chapter Fifteen
Retracing the Past

When T.J. graduated from high school, the United States had just gotten out of the Korean War. Despite the fact that there were no battles being waged at that time, we did not have an all-volunteer army and eighteen-year-old males still had to report to some branch of the armed forces for service. T.J. knew nothing about the differences between each branch, other than knowing he had to join one of them. He decided to enlist in the Marine Corps, not because he wanted to be one of "The Few, the Proud" but because he liked their uniforms.

Gladys reported that the recruiting officer told her husband that T.J. made the highest mark of anyone they had in Virginia—a high #2—the highest being #1, which was a genius and they hadn't had anyone with that rating.

The Marine Corps ignited his insatiable appetite to explore other countries. In a letter to Gladys, T.J. touched on his infatuation with Japan and wondered if it was past-life related.

"I wish it were possible for you and [...] to visit Japan—it's such an amazing country," he wrote. "They're such brave, polite people, living in such poverty—the larger percent anyway. You know, I've never seen a

Japanese child cry, always they laugh. I wonder what their secret is—maybe some day I shall find out. There's so terribly much to see. Once while visiting Kamishiro I saw the Buddha and Shinto Shrines. Have you ever seen a real Buddhist temple? It's really something to see. Are you sure I have never been Japanese or at least Mongolian? Say, wasn't Alexander the Great oriental? Oh well, I don't know why I feel so much at home here with these people. I can speak Japanese almost as well as English."

When his enlistment was over, he didn't know what to do other than to continue traveling so he could visit all the places that Mr. Cayce said they had lived during their previous lives. He only had one problem and that was how to pay for it. He took on whatever odd jobs he could find, including being a lifeguard at the beach. He had a few friends who basically were in the same boat. They called themselves the East Coast Power Team and together came up with ideas for making money. Sometimes they would make things to sell to tourists during the summer and then when the tourist season was over, they'd all go someplace together, usually to Florida.

One summer T.J. got especially inventive. He had a friend in the Village in New York City who sold him hundreds of dresses for a mere 40 cents each. T.J. brought them back to the Boardwalk and started a business called "Dresses A Go Go." He made thousands of dollars that summer.

His friend Robert came up with the idea that rather than go to Florida again, the group should visit a place they had never been to before. They decided that each of them would buy a ticket to someplace in the world and not tell the others where it was. Then they would put on blindfolds and draw a ticket out of a hat. Wherever it was, that's where they would go. T.J. drew the ticket to Luxembourg, a place he had never heard of before. Still, believing all things have a purpose, he used the ticket and boarded the flight to that tiny country in Western Europe.

When he landed, he saw a marquis with what he hoped would have a list of destinations so he could get out of that country and into one he was more familiar with, but the sign was written in what he described as a combination of French and German which he could not decipher.

"While I stood there, trying to figure out what it said, I realized I had no idea what I was doing there," he recalled. "I couldn't talk to anyone and I couldn't read anything. I continued to stand there, staring at the sign, with people going around me, not really paying much attention to my dilemma. I must have stood there for at least ten minutes when a guy around my age tapped me on the shoulder and said, 'You can't read any of that, can you?'"

"No," I answered. "I can speak Japanese and a few other languages, but I have absolutely no idea what this says."

"Where do you want to go?" he asked.

"Well, that's another thing. I don't know that. I have no destination planned. I just want to go somewhere cool."

"Look, I'm Greek," he said. "I go to NYU and I'm going home to Thessaloniki. Why don't you come to Greece? It's a great country. You can hang out with me, my parents and my sister and two cousins. We all live in this great house. There's plenty of room. Stay with us for a few days until you get oriented and see where you want to go and we'll help you out."

"He didn't have to ask me twice. I said, 'Yeah, let's go' and the next thing I know I'm on a plane heading to Greece."

What his new friend did not tell him was that his father was the mayor of Thessaloniki, which was the capital of Greece at the time.

"Like Gracie Mansion in New York, the house they lived in was given to the mayor and his family as their residence while he was in office," T.J. said. "This was no ordinary house. It was ancient and had once belonged to Aristotle and was the very place where Aristotle had tutored—you got it—Alexander. So there I was, living in the same house I had once known so well in a previous lifetime. I started paying close attention to what was going on around me because I had a feeling this was just the beginning of one of the most divinely orchestrated periods of my life."

T.J. was welcomed with open arms and the two months he spent there was an extraordinary time for him. The people in that neighborhood treated him like he was a god.

"Of course, I never said anything like, 'Hi, I'm Alexander and I used to be the king here,' but you would not have known that by the way they treated me. I felt totally loved and accepted there. After a while, I began to think I really was Greek."

T.J. experienced some past-life bleed through during the time he spent in that house, including some rather vivid dreams about dying at thirty-three—the age that Alexander died.

"I also learned that my friend, the young man who tapped me on the shoulder and brought me to his home, had been Hephaestion, a Macedonian nobleman and general in Alexander's army. He had been brought up with Alexander and was considered his dearest friend."

Despite his love of Greece, living in Aristotle's house with a dear friend from his past life, and having the love of the people in the village, T.J. kept having dreams about Mr. Cayce in which Cayce would say, "You have to get out of here. This is not the place for you. Hit the road."

So that's what he did. He had a little money left and he decided to go to Italy. He did not recall ever living there before, but he loved the country's history, the art, and he especially liked the architecture. He got on a ferry in Greece that took him to Brindisi, an Italian coastal town. From there he caught a train heading to Rome. He decided to get off at Perugia to explore that town.

"Perugia is a fascinating town, with a city beneath a city, cobblestone streets and little places where you could get a torch and carry it around on your walk at night," he said.

One day he was walking down the street when he heard someone call out his name. At first he thought he was imagining it, because he didn't think anyone in Perugia knew who he was, but the voice persisted. He turned around and there was a friend of his who was the drummer in a trio he had been in. They enlisted in the Marine Corps around the same time and consequently got out around the same time. There he was sitting on the piazza drinking a bottle of wine and smoking a cigarette.

"T.J., what's up?" he asked after they greeted each other.

"Man, how are you doing?" T.J. replied. "What are you doing here?"

"I'm going to school. Why don't you go to school here with me?"

"I don't have any money," T.J. said. "I have maybe four to five thousand dollars and that's my travel money. After that I have to go home and get a job or go to school or something in Virginia Beach where I can afford it."

T.J. was surprised to hear his friend was going to school in Italy because he never had any money and T.J. wondered how in the world he could afford it, so he asked him.

"We have the G.I. bill," his friend answered somewhat astonished that T.J. didn't know about it. "You can go to school. They'll give you money. They pay for the place where you live. They buy you food. Pay for your books. Give you a little money to spend. And they do it for four years! There's a great school here. Why don't you come to school here?"

"So I thought—go to school for free? I will get all that money and stay in Perugia for four years? That was almost unbelievable. So taking his advice, I went over to the Universitâ per Stranieri, one of the oldest universities in Europe, registered and was accepted."

The next day he began looking for a place to live. As he was walking down the street, he saw a pensione, which he described as a little apartment building where you rent out individual rooms. He went in there and they were full, but the man told him that he should go next door and talk to the woman there because she rented out the top of her house to students. So he went there and saw a "For Rent" sign on the top floor.

"I knocked on the door and Senora Brute comes to the door. I introduced myself, told her I was from 'Stati Uniti' America, and that I was going to school there and looking for a place to live. She said, 'Oh good, good. I have a place. Let me show you.'"

She invited him in and showed him the apartment on the roof overlooking the field where all the soccer games were played. He really liked soccer and could see himself sitting up there looking down on all the soccer games, so he agreed to take the place.

She asked him if he'd like to have some refreshments and he accepted her gracious offer. When she went to the kitchen to brew some espresso, he went into the living room and sat down. He began looking around the room and saw a piano that was filled with photographs of what he perceived to be her entire family. He read enough about the culture to know that when you are a stranger in someone's home, you have to look at all the photos on display.

"I got up and began to look at each of the photographs," he recalled. "Then I came to one that stopped me dead in my tracks. It was a photograph of my childhood friend, Stefanella; complete with her little violin case! I stared at the photo, almost in near disbelief. It did not totally freak me out because after all, I had seen fairies and experienced Mr. Cayce reading my mind and everything that went along with that. So I'm thinking to myself—what is going on here? Senora Brute came back into the room and could clearly see I was perplexed.

"Who is this little girl?" T.J. asked pointing to the picture. "I know her. Her name is Stefanella Bersante."

"Yes, yes. How do you know her?" Senora Brute asked.

"I met her when I was a little kid," T.J. answered.

Right away T.J. realized that he stuck his foot in the wrong place. Knowing Senora Brute was Catholic, he did not want to tell her that he knew her relative because his mentor conjured her up. Not wanting to deceive her, however, he cautiously explained the story, admitting that he wouldn't blame her if she thought he was a bit crazy. He was relieved when she didn't throw him out, but instead was intrigued by his story. She appeared to be excited and said she felt as though he was related to her.

She allowed T.J. to live there, free of charge, for four years. On top of that, she cooked dinner for him every night. He played the cello and she played the piano. Sometimes he worked in her garden, half expecting Stefie to show up, but she never did. Still he always felt as though Stefanella was around somewhere.

While T.J. attended school, he studied architecture, medieval art, and perfected his Italian, but he did not end up with a degree. He stayed in school so he could live in Perugia until the money ran out. The university was full of people from all over Europe, Africa, and the Middle East. There weren't many Americans there, but a few students were from Great Britain. T.J. liked most of them and thought they were cool.

There was one fellow in particular who made life especially interesting. He was an actual count named Carlio, so T.J. said he had a swagger attitude to begin with.

"In Italy that's a big deal, especially in Perugia with all their hierarchy," T.J. said. "Carlio liked me and I liked him."

One day Carlio asked T.J. if he wanted to go to Rome to hang out. T.J. agreed and got into Carlio's Jeep. Carlio said, "Let's go see what's going on at the Vatican." T.J. thought that was cool because he had read a lot about the Vatican and going with someone like him, who he thought may have connections, would give him an insight into what was going on inside the Vatican.

"Unfortunately, Carlio had been drinking wine

and by the time we got there, he was inebriated," T.J. recalled. "He drove up the Vatican steps and right past the Vatican Secret Service. I could see they knew him. They made us stop and Carlio got up and left. He went into the Vatican and just walked by these guys. They didn't mess with him because he was a count, but there I was, stuck in the Jeep so they came and got me for trespassing. One of them said, 'If you're trespassing and you're hanging out with Carlio, you're going to have to go to the Vatican jail until we straighten this out.'"

They took T.J. into a small room occupied by priests. "It was like being in the third precinct in NYC except they all had robes on with rosary beads," he said.

He stayed there for about a half hour and finally Carlio came down, took the keys off the table, opened the door, let T.J. out, and they left. By that time T.J. was scared to death, convinced they were going to come after them, but they never did. After that T.J. never went anywhere with Carlio.

T.J. was living at a hotel for a while toward the end of his stay in Italy. On the second or third night he was there, he noticed a little coffee bar.

"Perugia's underground hung out there and I got to meet all the locals," he said. "It was like going to an old Boys Club in Manhattan, but these were men and women. A woman I knew by the name of Maria had a father who was in the Roman Senate, so they were all kids of big shots. They asked me where I was from and I said Virginia Beach and they all knew Edgar Cayce. They were having séances and playing with the Quija Board. They asked if I wanted to go to the séance and I agreed. I walked in and there was a long table they sat around trying to conjure up spirits. I told them that would not work. I explained that they had to be careful what they were asking for because you don't know whom you're going to get—maybe Mussolini would come back to clear up some things. I said they shouldn't settle for any run-of-the-mill spirit but should go to the headman. I suggested we meditate and ask for guidance. If you're going to ask for somebody who's not alive anymore, why don't you try Jesus Christ?

"They just looked at me. Maria was at the head of the table. I don't know if we connected with Christ or not, but the medium said he and Christ walked in a garden and the way is, SEARCH FOR GOD. They were flabbergasted because they were all Catholics. So after that we started a SEARCH FOR GOD group. I doubt if they ever finished it, but they thought it was pretty interesting."

During summer vacation, people would invite T.J. to their homes while he looked for work. The first summer he went back to Greece and ended up on Mykonos. There he got a job as a disc jockey in a discotheque that was in an old windmill. The disco had American records but they didn't have anyone who could read the titles, so he got the job.

On the way to Mykonos, T.J. met some guys on the boat who, like T.J., needed a place to live. They eventually found a place they could afford and lived there for a few months. Unfortunately, T.J. didn't know them well enough to know they were heavy marijuana users.

"So we're in the house and everybody's puffing up and smoke is going out the window," T.J. recalled. "There's this knock on the door. It's a guy who's the combination mayor, chief of police, and ran the only newspaper in town. He brought us all out front to check our passports. At that time, I had really long hair. So he's standing there looking at my passport and then at me.

"Thomas Jefferson? I heard this name before. Is he a writer?"

"A very famous writer," I answered. "That's me."

And so he said, "I want you to write about me."

"'Of course,' I answered, thinking this was my way of avoiding arrest. The last thing I wanted was to be hauled off to his little dinky jail that was about a foot wide."

He let T.J. off with the understanding that he would write about him. T.J. went through the motions and went over to his house on the pretext of interviewing him. Sometimes he was acting in the capacity as the mayor and he wore a sash, so T.J. would take his picture with his sash or sometimes of him wearing his police outfit. Every time T.J. saw him, he'd take his picture and pretend he was writing something down about him. Luckily, T.J. left before the man asked to see the finished product.

T.J.'s karmic connections never seemed far behind during the years he traveled. He recalled one night when he was walking home in the rain from a coffee shop in Paris. He saw a church nearby and sat on the steps to get out of the rain. He described the church as looking like a 7-11 with a cross on it. He looked up at the name of the church and later when he got back home, he told Gladys about it. She said, "Oh I used to be a nun in that church in a previous lifetime."

Many of the relationships that he began in Virginia Beach had strands that stretched overseas in some unusual ways. A lot of people came to the Beach because of Mr. Cayce, many of whom were T.J.'s age. He became friends with many people because he was looked upon as an incarnated rock star in those days. That's how he met Achmed.

"He and his family would come to the Beach and during the summer I would go to Egypt and stay with them at their home right outside of Cairo," T.J. said. "They had an interesting past. For hundreds of generations, they had been custodians of the Giza pyramids. Achmed's grandfather sold and rented camels, like a used-car dealership. They were mostly plow camels—not people camels. When I would visit Achmed in Egypt, we would hang out with the camels and I got pretty good with handling and riding them. Achmed and I would gather up some food and go out in the desert and climb up the top of the pyramids and throw baseballs down to each other.

We'd wear old miner hats with a light on them and chase each other through the Giza pyramids. And then we'd ride up to Luxor, or go up into the Valley of the Kings. Or if we had enough of the desert, we'd get on an old boat and sail up the Nile. I felt like Lawrence of Arabia and learned to live like an Arab. I even could speak the language a little bit. It was an unbelievable time."

T.J. admitted having some trouble there because of his incarnation as Alexander.

"In essence, I had been their Pharaoh in a past life," T.J. said. "So Achmed was always letting me have the last seat or offering to help me with this or that, as if I were a king. I was constantly telling him to stop that, but he persisted. His whole family was wonderful."

T.J. did get into some trouble in Egypt, admitting it was out of his own stupidity.

"One time I had a bottle of wine and this really beautiful tablecloth I bought in Italy," he explained. "I packed my camel with a portable battery-powered record player, a Jimi Hendrix record, and a recording of Claire de Lune. Achmed and I rode into this little date palm oasis. There was no one around so I put out the tablecloth, started having wine, and smoked a little hashish. We were sitting there a little loaded from drinking and eating. Achmed no sooner said it was unusual that no one was there when all of a sudden this figure dashes between two of these little huts. He jumped out in front of us, waving one of those long curved knives. He looked really scary, rattling on and on. He was very upset that we were there, especially

Achmed because he was Egyptian. He knew right away that I was American. I'll never forget this man, as he had two thumbs on one hand. I can't remember his face, but I remember his hands—that knife and the two thumbs. Turns out he was just angry because of the wine. That was the only time I had a close call."

During this period of his life, T.J. traveled to nine different countries. When his travels were over, Gladys sent him a letter and informed him that he had taken the exact route that Alexander had taken—town for town—when he was out conquering the world.

"Somehow, I knew this, even before she said it," T.J. said. "I felt a lot of love when I went through some places. Other places they wanted to throw things at me, so I had to be careful wherever I went because I was aware that when I met people it could very well be that we had some kind of relationship from the past. Some of those relationships were good; some not so good."

Chapter Sixteen

So, Mr. Jefferson, What Have You Done Lately?

T.J. wearing Edgar Cayce's hat. Photo courtesy of John Aguilar.

When you are two days old and the greatest prophet of the twentieth century proclaims that you can do for the world what Thomas Jefferson did for this country, the odds are stacked against you from the start. What soul—no matter how lofty—can live with that burden? In considering that reading, T.J. always has said that had Mr. Cayce lived long enough to see him reach adulthood, perhaps T.J. would have had the tools to at least give saving the world a shot. Instead, he was lost in what he perceived to be a hostile world that fueled his rebellious side.

"I became the karmic poster child for souls who had achieved greatness in the past but who were incapable of accomplishing anything other than using people to get through life," T.J. said. "That is the reputation I developed—of someone who was irresponsible, lazy, and troubled." His reputation spread like a contagion and soon he found many people, some who did not know him personally, believing he was a freeloader and a source of embarrassment to the organization that his mentor founded—"only because I went off the deep end and hadn't achieved what he predicted."

T.J. admits he never had any clear direction. "I had no idea what I was capable of doing, or where to focus my energies, and because I had been ridiculed for years about my beliefs, I struggled to find something—anything—that I could call my own," he said.

There were some interests that had staying power, but unfortunately none had anything to do with Cayce's prediction. Fast, expensive sports cars were an obsession.

Burlynn noted that T.J. was trying to save enough money to buy a Mercedes Benz, a car he called "the greatest in foreign cars." It wasn't until he was in his seventies that he was able to buy a used Mercedes, but that didn't last long as he claims the man he hired to repair the car ended up stealing it.

Ironically, there was an article in a local Charlottesville paper that was speculating on what type of car Thomas Jefferson would own if he were alive today, and some guessed it would be a Mercedes. In reality, after the Mercedes was stolen, he ended up driving an old beat-up Toyota truck. Not very presidential, but it got him where he needed to go.

Music has always been one of T.J.'s passions. As a baby he liked to listen to music on the radio, including opera. He played the coronet in a school band and later learned to play the bass fiddle after very little instruction. He especially loved jazz and attended every jazz concert he could find. In Los Angeles, he played in a combo band making records and filling in engagements in nightspots around town. Later he worked in a hotel during the day and played in a jazz quintet at night. "I loved music so much that I hoped to go to college and major in music, hoping to teach music someday," he said. "That never happened either."

T.J. loved art as much as he loved music. The little stick-like drawings he did as a child fill his file at ECF. There were times he'd be sketching out a lifelike drawing in school and get in trouble because he wasn't paying attention to the instructor. Gladys said that after he enlisted in the Marine Corps, she found many of those drawings in his room, including one that was a perfect likeness of Harry S. Truman. She said he had a real knack for catching facial expressions.

Gladys said he rekindled his love of art while on vacation in 1963 and spent every spare minute painting. He took an art course once a week and his teacher said he showed extraordinary talent. For several months he spent most of his time in an artist colony and enjoyed a bohemian type of life. He helped establish a cooperative community project that included a leather shop, arts and crafts gift shop, clothing, and more.

"My intent was to promote creativity and soul development among young people, but as with all my other jobs—that did not last," he said.

His love of art fed his love of reading. While on that same vacation, he began combing libraries and reading everything he could on art, but also on philosophy. He especially liked Gibran, Dostoyevsky, and Tolstoy and sought out people he could talk with concerning such things. It was as if he developed an insatiable appetite for learning.

T.J. had jobs in more fields than he could count. One summer he spent an enjoyable three months as a lifeguard. He worked in the fashion industry, including selling shoes, managing a clothing store and a boutique. He wrote and sold commercials for radio and television programs, a job he loved as it gave him the opportunity to travel.

The closest that T.J. came to working with the Cayce material was when he was a clerk at the Heritage Store, a local health food store in Virginia Beach that sold Cayce remedies. His last job was roasting coffee beans for Greenberry's Coffee Company in Charlottesville.

No matter what career direction he explored, he knew something was missing. "What could compare to being about Mr. Cayce's work?" he asked. "I wanted to share all I had learned from my mentor. That is how I envisioned I would spend my entire professional life. Consequently, I never found a career in the private or public sector that held my attention for any length of time."

Just as he could not find passion for a career, so too, he was unable to find lasting happiness with the many women who came into his life. He married several times and had multiple affairs and acknowledged he wasn't much of a father until later in life.

"Like my father before me who tried but had no success as a parent, I admit I was not a good father to my older children," he said. "It was only when my two youngest daughters were born and I became a house husband and raised them that I finally understood what parental love was all about."

Throughout his life, T.J. was able to apply lessons he learned from his years as Cayce's protégé. One of the most valuable—and the one that has served him throughout his life—was his lesson in healthy living. Although the readings indicate he experienced more than his share of health issues as a child, T.J. makes the claim that until recently, he has never been seriously ill in his entire adult life. The only time he got a bit of a cold was when he would get cocky and said, "I've never had a cold" and then he'd manifest a minor sore throat. The majority of the readings that Mr. Cayce gave were health readings, so it stood to reason he would teach T.J. how to stay well.

The first health lesson T.J. recalled had to do with his thoughts. Cayce instructed T.J. that thoughts were important and that he needed to be careful what came into his mind. "He said a person who is constantly thinking negative thoughts is building an image of negativity and that, in turn, attracts negativity and you find yourself dealing with things like flat tires, bankruptcy, whatever," T.J. recalled. "He showed me how important it was to manage my negative thoughts."

The next health lesson was how to eat—to ingest one thing that grows below the ground and three things that grow above the ground. T.J. said he was told those were all things that were compatible in digestion. By eating this way, you get all the minerals that work together that you need for growth.

The other lesson had to do with glyco-thymoline. "It's actually a mouthwash but what I do is take a little cup and put a small amount of glyco in the bottom and fill the rest with water and I sip it all day, especially when I feel as though I might be catching a cold," T.J. said. "What that does is make your system alkaline. Most germs or viruses can't live in an alkaline environment. They need an acidic stomach to live and grow in. This will kill any virus. When Mr. Cayce gave me the glyco, the procedure was I would take aspirin and get my antibodies ready to roll and then I'd sip the glyco and I would get well."

A lot of what T.J. learned about healing came from watching the people who came to see Cayce. Many of them were dying. They had been to multiple doctors who just scratched their heads and had no idea how to help them. These people would end up at Cayce's home as a last resort. T.J. said Cayce had a few friends who were doctors and even they would send their patients to him for a reading.

"Mr. Cayce always came through for them," T.J. said. "He not only would tell the person how to heal, but he also told them why they were in this shape, which always had to do with karma. He believed if you don't fix the cause of the illness you're not going to fix the effect either. In the fourteen thousand plus total readings he gave, the majority of which were health readings, he was never wrong."

T.J. said today if he has a question, even if it's about his aching foot, he could find answers in the readings. Throughout his life, he has been able to fix almost any problem that's come up, simply by referencing the readings.

"I don't mean to say it as if I'm bragging," he clarified. "It's just that I have been able to treat myself by using glyco-thymoline and castor oil. I do all the things

I'm supposed to do. I eat well and even talk to my food before I eat it. There have been periods where I sloughed off a bit and did not stick to what he said about having good thoughts. Maybe I've had a couple of colds only because I was too lazy to do what I was supposed to do. But when I do everything he told me to do, I stay healthy. And that's the deal. Everyone can live for a long time. People in the Bible lived five hundred years. I always said I'd live to be one hundred and forty."

Considering that T.J. came into this world near death and Cayce's recommendation that he be given Carnation milk is what saved his life, it is interesting to see how T.J.'s childhood health was something of interest to so many people.

The use of alcohol was a serious issue for both of his parents, and while their drinking caused problems for T.J. when he was a baby, it did not plant the seed of alcoholism in him at all.

"You may be wondering if having parents as alcoholics led me to have a drinking problem as well and the answer is no," T.J. explained. "I don't drink alcohol. I admit to trying to drink as a teenager—what healthy American teenager doesn't—but I got so sick that I never tried again."

Even Gladys noted that in a letter she wrote on June 10, 1964, in which she commented about T.J.'s health. "It is interesting to note that after going through his teens in perfect health, while in the Marines it was discovered that he had a stomach ulcer. Every now and then the trouble flares up and needs to be treated, sometimes requiring hospitalization. Fortunately, no surgery has yet been performed. Another interesting thing to me is that he has never been able to drink alcoholic beverages. As he first began to try, in his early teens, he would become deathly ill, vomiting, etc."

T.J. laments the fact that nothing turned out the way he hoped. "The bottom line is that there *was* a plan and that I was part of the plan. The plan was to save the world. That's what Mr. Cayce tried to do—to come here and show people how to be loving and creative. I was meant to continue to do that and perhaps in doing so, fulfill the destiny he proclaimed for me when I was a few days old."

T.J. considers Gladys and Edgar as a guiding force in his life, even to this day. "She and Mr. Cayce appear in my dreams, trying to help me out. If it weren't for their angelic presence in my life, I would be a mess. What I do know is that had Mr. Cayce lived long enough to help implement the plan the readings suggested about me, things would have been a lot different. But when he died, I was too young to understand much about destiny, much less think there was anything I could do about it."

As he looked back on their many conversations, T.J. remembered bits and pieces of talks that alluded to his future work. "One time I asked Mr. Cayce if when he was my age, if he ever thought of growing up to be a person who gave readings. He said no, but then he turned the question to me and asked what I wanted to do when I grew up. Since I idolized the man, I told him I wanted to do the exact same thing he was doing. He said he didn't know if I could do exactly what he was doing, but he did say he hoped I always would be an important part of the A.R.E. His vision for the future of the A.R.E. included me. Of that I am certain."

Gladys believed that as well, feeling that if T.J. and Hugh Lynn's son, Charles Thomas, worked together, they could accomplish great things. Writing to Boyd in August 1944, she described the positive traits each boy exhibited.

> Little Chas. Thomas Cayce is a charmer—
> he makes friends everywhere and everyone
> loves him. Thos. Jeff. always made friends
> with everybody by talking and never
> meeting a stranger, by being a handshaking
> politician in other words, but little Chas.
> Thos. just looks at people and smiles and
> they fall over themselves to get at him. It
> certainly is going to be interesting to watch
> these youngsters grow up and maybe have
> a part in helping them find expression.
> Eckin's baby is just as cute as he can be but
> as different from Chas. Thom. as Eckin is
> different from H.L. If we can have a part in
> bringing all these great souls together with
> one spiritual ideal, even though their lines
> of material expression may be millions

of miles apart, we will have served our purpose in being associated with them, I think.

One wonders what would have happened had Gladys's vision come true. What is certain, however, is that for T.J., not having a job at the A.R.E. was as disappointing as not attending the High Mowing School. At one point, Gladys asked T.J. to stop applying for work there because it was hurtful for her to see him so disappointed.

"Over the years, I must have tried a million times to work there," he said. "After all, I had been taught everything. I read every one of those fourteen thousand readings, so I knew I'd be good to work there. All of those years of Mr. Cayce tutoring me on the pier and pouring all that wisdom into my heart and soul, I wanted to get that information out to people. Yet fate was such that I never had the opportunity of sharing any of that with others on the path. I may not have a role in the A.R.E. as Mr. Cayce hoped, but what I do have are the truths he imparted to me during our brief time together. I see what is going on and the only thing I know that could put a dent in this is if people realized what karma is because you don't get away with anything. Karma is not just a word that's in a song. Karma is big time. You hurt somebody and you come back the next time, you better realize you're coming back to meet yourself. What we have to concentrate on as human beings is love. We have to get our thinking right. We have to think good thoughts about people. We have to realize that we were created in a positive way, not a negative way. We weren't created to be a world of Satans. We were created in the image of God, the creator. We have to understand that we have to become selfless people, not selfish. Selfish is the killer. You become selfish and you treat everybody in a negative way. You become a negative person.

"And I didn't even start trying to be good until I was about twenty-five. Before that it didn't really matter to me. I was so wiped out about whom I was and what was going on, I never considered it. But it was always in the back of my mind. I knew that things had to change here because there was too much bad stuff. I know within myself that our planet is in big trouble. That to me is on my shoulders. I feel I know enough to straighten this out, but I don't know how to get people's attention. I know what to tell people that it's a possibility if you want your grandchildren and your grandchildren's grandchildren to live here, this is what we have to do.

"We have come thousands of years and things are no better now than they were back in Atlantis. Where does that leave us? It leaves us to start over again maybe, unless we can stop it. Because that's what happened in Atlantis. The whole thing fell apart and we had to rebuild and we didn't learn anything.

"One of the most important lessons Mr. Cayce taught me was that anything is possible because we have a creative God, not a destructive God, and we have to pay attention to what that loving force does. More than anything, I want to help get people together and raise the planet's vibration by knowing what God is. Just as in Atlantis, I want to convert souls from the Sons of Belial to the Law of One. We have to get our thinking right and realize that we were created in a positive way, not in a negative way. We were created in the image of God, the Creator. So, we have to understand that we have to become selfless—not selfish—people because selfishness will destroy the planet. This isn't to say there aren't good people in this world who are trying to do the right thing— there are, but everyone has to pull together. The common denominator has to be love, not greed. That's where our roots are, in love. That's how we were created. Until we learn to use our heritage, which is love and kindness, we're not going to accomplish anything. I don't have a wealth of information. I'm not a scholar, but I do know that we are one, and if we are one, then we are a lot like God the Creator and who best to align yourself with than the big chief?"

Afterword

In the years following Cayce's death, the Davis family continued to contend with problems Cayce tried to resolve during his lifetime, but to no avail. While no one will ever know what path their lives may have taken had Cayce lived longer and given T.J. that all-important second life reading, we do know what happened to this family in the years following Cayce's demise. These highlights, taken from the reports in the readings of T.J., his parents, and Gladys, tell their own story.

Within a few months after Mr. Cayce died, Burlynn's companion died suddenly of a heart attack. She subsequently sold her restaurant and remarried Boyd, who had returned from the army. Gladys reported it was a very brief marriage, only about a month, as "they both were wallowing in self-pity and self-indulgence; drink had gotten the best of them."

By 1947, Burlynn was still floundering, trying to find work. The money she had received from the sale of the restaurant was running out. She married again but that marriage did not last very long either. Over the next two years—the important twelfth and thirteenth years of T.J.'s life—were especially chaotic with constant changes and moves.

Boyd meanwhile continued to skip from one job to another—from Alabama to San Antonio to Seattle and back to Virginia. In 1949 he was diagnosed with tuberculosis and for the rest of his life spent months at a time in and out of a veteran's hospital.

After Gladys married Al Turner in 1952, T.J. continued to live with them while his parents dealt with their ongoing health issues. Boyd contracted pleurisy while Burlynn suffered from fibroid tumors, asthma, and arthritis.

Boyd's life added yet another tragic chapter when he married Elizabeth (Beth) Harley Graves on August 9, 1956. Like his marriage to Burlynn, his relationship with Beth was fraught with problems. In April 1957 Boyd was in an A.A. home in Los Angeles, hoping to remain there until he could stop his drinking for good and get a better-paying job. He wanted Beth to join him in California, while she wanted him to return to Virginia. But a month later, Beth was dead.

According to Gladys: "She was found in her car in garage, no gas, dead battery, ignition on, closed doors, indicating she had got in car, started motor and passed out."

Most thought it was suicide, but Gladys, Al, and others were convinced it was accidental. Al sent details to Boyd, encouraging him to remain sober. He also wrote to T.J., who, at the time, was in the service stationed in San

Francisco. Al encouraged T.J. to send his condolences to Boyd, saying their father-son relationship may be upside down to T.J., but he'd have to take the place of comforter to Boyd, who had suffered "a dreadful shock."

For his part, Boyd never gave up hope that he and Burlynn could make a go of their lives. During 1959, he and Burlynn discussed getting together again. Boyd began sending her almost all of his pension money, but said it wasn't enough while he was in the hospital so he decided to leave and get a job. Burlynn was supposed to meet him in Yellowstone, but she had car trouble and never showed up. He then arranged to meet her in Denver, but after learning she had spent all the money he sent, he decided to hitchhike back to Los Angeles and go on without her. He eventually made his way to Miami where he found a good-paying job, still hopeful Burlynn would join him someday.

Reflecting on the roller-coaster relationship he and Burlynn were on from day one, Boyd felt pangs of guilt where T.J. was concerned. Wanting to make sense of it, he expressed his perspective of the situation. "I'm sure that if your mother and I had stayed together I could have done as well as any of the guys around the beach. Whose fault it was is of no consequence. It's probably better that we did separate. We are both pretty stubborn and have violent tempers at times. . . . I know that both of us would have wanted you to have a much nicer life than you did have but our own little petty likes and dislikes at the time were all important. Now they don't seem to be, but it's too late as far as you are concerned. The time when we both should have been with you, we were somewhere else. You know all this, but I want you to know that I know and realize it too and it has done me much more harm than you, I'm sure."

Boyd and Burlynn would never reconcile again. Her health continued to deteriorate and by 1978 she was on welfare. By then she was living in Ohio, depressed and lonely. She called Gladys in July of 1978, telling her she had a vision of a white-robed lady holding out her hand to her. Gladys told her she thought it was a wonderful vision that meant she was going to receive her healing, but shortly thereafter, on July 17 at 10:40 p.m., Burlynn died alone in an ambulance on the way to the hospital.

For Boyd, bad luck was always around the corner. A month after leaving the T.B. hospital in August 1957, everything he owned was stolen from his apartment while he spent the night with a friend. All he had left were the clothes on his back.

T.J. returned to Virginia Beach in 1959 and a year later married his first (of three) wives. His wedding prompted both Boyd and Burlynn to reconsider reconciliation yet again. Gladys wrote: "They attempted to 'make up' but it was no good."

After his first marriage failed, T.J. began to lead a vagabond existence, following art and jazz festivals and neglecting his appearance. Even so, Gladys maintained her belief in him, writing: "Such great possibilities are apparent, if only he could find the incentive to stick to a definite purpose long enough to succeed with it."

T.J. remarried in 1966 but two years later, he and his wife separated and were subsequently divorced. Each of his two marriages had produced a son, so now T.J. had two boys of his own.

Boyd remarried in 1961 and settled in Los Angeles. In 1963, he got a job as a hotel desk clerk but after three months had to stop because his T.B. became active again. Two years later he reported suffering from stomach ulcers caused by taking the T.B. drugs for so long. That was compounded with his being diagnosed with emphysema, which made it difficult for him to breathe at times.

Boyd and his wife separated in the fall of 1964 and he reentered a T.B. hospital in Florida. He was in and out of the hospital in 1965. Two years later, his ex-wife phoned Gladys to ask if she had heard from him as the health department said he had gone AWOL and was still active. Boyd admitted he tested positive again, adding that the doctor at the clinic said he had two cavities in his lungs the size of a half dollar. Boyd anticipated he'd be in the hospital for at least another year. He died on April 9, 1983, in California Veterans Nursing Home.

T.J. remarried a third time and had two daughters by this marriage. He ultimately moved to Charlottesville, Virginia, fulfilling Mr. Cayce's advice that he return to where he lived during the Jefferson lifetime.

As for the trajectory of his life, it could best be summed up in a small segment of a written analysis of T.J. by one of the cofounders of the coop he helped form back in 1966. It is almost prophetic about the direction T.J.'s life was taking.

" . . . So as to the Law of Love - we love him dearly for what he is, for what is obvious to all that he can be. And we have compassion for him for what he has let himself become and seems so inextricably bound to by choice and desire and fear. But we can't allow that person to work with us to become known as us. He is not a representative of us, only of himself. We cannot carry his weight. We cannot lift him physically and act as puppeteers, controlling his actions and words. He has to act from himself, as an individual, for we are not manipulators or puppeteers. Each has his own being to guide, to choose for, and to advance. We develop our own individually as regard to Self and to purpose, which is to manifest the ideal of human existence on the earth plane. We cannot coerce or force or manipulate - each must make his own decision all along the way, and he has his own free will to choose, advance, follow, lead, or leave at any point along the way."

This is how others saw him—and continue to see him today. Yet this is a book about choices. About a soul's mission that went awry. Separating the ego from the soul consciousness, it is only fair to end this book with words coming from T.J.'s truest and highest self. This is, after all, the essence of his soul and if judgment should be forthcoming, let what he wrote in a letter to Harmon Bro in April 1970 be entered into his Akashic Record:

So let us believe in tomorrow. Also, the shadow of our lives never goes away. Do we not belong to each other, all of us, every single twig and branch, brook and ocean, are we not one great consciousness of the unity of all life? I think we are... Then that makes love the most important thing in the universe. I say let us believe in love for it is the only way we have. The strength, then, of being positive in the face of good is always easy. But, what of the strength of positive in the hungry face of sin, failure, stubbing your toe, teasing a crippled mind. That is the test of love, patience, the way of light, the Light!

About the Author

Ask Joanne DiMaggio, MA, CHt, what is her soul's purpose and she answers with a smile: "I am a reporter for the Universe." Joanne says writing is a part of her spiritual DNA and sees her soul's mission in this life to observe, record and disseminate information about her particular area of espertise in esoteric studies: soul writing and past-life exploration,

A professional writer and author of five books and hundreds of magazine articles for both mainstream and esoteric audiences, in 1987 she began devoting all of her time to her esoteric studies, specializing in past-life exploration, research and therapy. She eventually combined her passion for soul writing with her knowledge of reincarnation and today is considered a respected expert in both fields.

Born and raised in Chicago, Joanne has been actively involved with Edgar Cayce's Association for Research and Enlightenment (A.R.E.) since 1987. In 1990, she became one of the founding members of the A.R.E. Heartland Region headquartered in Chicago. There she oversaw the region's public relations, newsletter, and special event programming. She moved to Charlottesville, Virginia in 1995 and has been the Coordinator for the A.R.E. Charlottesville, VA team since August 2008.

Joanne earned her Masters in Transpersonal Studies degree through Atlantic University. Her thesis on inspirational writing served as the basis of her first esoteric book: *Soul Writing: Conversing with your Higher Self.* She also earned her Spiritual Metor certification through Atlantic University, where she was named Outstanding Graduate of the year. She later formed A.U.'s Alumni Association, which she served as a president for two years.

Joanne has given talks on the subject of past-life exploration and soul writing to audiences throughout the Chicago, IL area; in Austin, TX; Milwaukee, WI; Durham, NC; DeGray Lake, AR; the Washington DC area; and throughout Virginia. She also has made many presentations at Unity churches. In addition, Joanne has been the guest on nearly 90 national and international radio programs, including Coast to Coast AM and the Shirley Maclaine Show.

Joanne has been professionally pursuing past-life research and therapy for over 30 years. She is a graduate of the Eastern Institute of Hypnotherapy, completed additional training in hypnosis at the College of DuPage in Glen Ellyn, IL and studied under Dr. Irene Hickman, a pioneer in the field of non-directive hypnotherapy. The years she spent as the head of her own past-life research center enabled her to interact with some of the leading past-life therapists, authors, and other renowned practitioners from across the country.

Using soul writing, Joanne produced a small line of greeting cards called Spirit Song. The International Greeting Card Association cited one of those cards, *What is Human is Immortal,* for its creative excellence, choosing it as one of six worldwide finalists in the "Sympathy" category for its Annual LOUIE Awards.

In addition to *Soul Writing,* her other esoteric books include *Your Soul Remembers: Accessing Your Past Lives Through Soul Writing* and *Karma Can Be a Real Pain: Past Life Clues to Current Life Maladies.* All are available on Amazon.

Contact Info:

www.joannedimaggio.com
joanne@joannedimaggio.com

OZARK
MOUNTAIN
PUBLISHING

For more information about any of the titles published by Ozark Mountain Publishing, Inc., soon to be released titles, or other items in our catalog, write, phone or visit our website:

Ozark Mountain Publishing, Inc.

PO Box 754

Huntsville, AR 72740

479-738-2348/800-935-0045

www.ozarkmt.com